Presentation Training A-Z

D1263906

BONUS MATERIAL

Register your copy of *Presentation Training A-Z* and receive helpful online materials.

Including:
- Video Instruction
- Audio Downloads
- Updates
- And More

www.presentationtraininga-z.com/register/

Testimonials for
Media Training Worldwide

"TJ Walker was able to help my entire team operate more efficiently [and] maximize their message penetration to their audience. I can tell you his pace was incredible, he was extremely articulate and he got the whole group involved. We really enjoyed the day."

– Michael Gallant
EMC

"Jess' information helped me gain a fresh perspective on image, content, speaking patterns and the impact of getting my message out."

– Linwood J. Oglesby
Newark Arts Council

"I put the skills learned to excellent use. I was told by the producer that it was refreshing to work with someone who was comfortable in front of the camera and could get their message points out. So, kudos to you for training me! It was a wonderful experience."

– Roxanne Moster
UCLA

"The training has helped greatly in terms of staying on message and in focus. The likelihood of being quoted has been greatly enhanced by following some basic tents."

– Jim Hudak
CIT Group

"I feel confident and more organized in my thought process."

– Ken Porter
TransUnion

"It has helped my confidence in delivering a message and greatly improved my ability to develop stories that explain key points."

– Keith Jacoby
Wachovia Securities

"I was particularly pleased with the way Media Training Worldwide customized my training session. They previewed and critiqued my videos and the trainer covered many topics never addressed for me in previous training sessions with other companies."

– Bonnie Taub-Dix
New York State Dietetic Association

"Jess helped me make my messages clear, concise, and helped ensure they reach my audience."

– Hala Haidar
AIG Lebanon

"The next day the phone started ringing. The local TV station wanted an interview... in 25 minutes!

I convened the same brain trust we used last time. In 20 minutes we had three message points. I dreamed up sound bites en route to the shooting location. The story was the lead on the evening news. Two of the three message points were run. One point had two sound bites attached.

Your training really paid off!

Thanks TJ!"

– Michael Hill
National Park Service

"TJ Walker is a great speaking expert and an effective and engaging teacher. He takes the fear factor out of speaking to the media and live audiences and clearly explains the secrets of great communicators like Reagan and Clinton. The best part is, what he teaches you really works when you put it to practice."

– Hakan Lindskog
TimeLife

Media Training Worldwide is known as an industry leader in the media and presentation training fields. The firm publishes more than 100 media and presentation training books, DVDs, CDs, and other information products.

TJ Walker & Jess Todtfeld are also the authors of:

- *Media Training A-Z (Book)*

- *How to Create More Effective PowerPoint Presentations (Special Report)*

- *Fear No More (CD)*

- *1001 Ways to Wow the Media and Speaking Audiences (Book)*

Presentation Training A-Z

A Complete Guide to Your Audience Understanding,
Remembering, Acting Upon and Telling Other People About
Your Message

By TJ Walker
&
Jess Todtfeld

MEDIA
TRAINING
WORLDWIDE

Published by **Media Training Worldwide**

Media Training Worldwide provides more media and presentation training workshops and seminars than any other company in the world. They also publish more than 100 media and presentation training books, DVDs, CDs, and other informational products making them the premier presentation/media training publisher in the world.

www.mediatrainingworldwide.com

Library of Congress Catalog Card Number: 2005920587
ISBN: 1-932642-39-0

Printed in the United States of America
First Printing: February 2006
Third Edition: October 2008

Developmental Editor: Kristin Boose
Copy Editor: Joni Mitchell
Cover Art: Adkins & Associates, INC
Book Design: Kristopher Gentile

This Book is Dedicated to
Audiences Around the World.
"May You Never Fall Asleep Again!"

Table Of Contents

Introduction

I have been coaching people on how to make better presentations for more than 20 years, and through my experiences, I've found that the majority of individuals share the same concerns. They want to be memorable, motivating, and mesmerizing speakers. I have also identified multiple myths that people tend to believe about giving presentations and facts that are perceived to be myths. As a coach and public speaker, I have found that there are many truths --and even some tricks-- to address these concerns. This book is a compilation of some of the insights I have learned along the way.

Why Give A Speech?

Why should you give a speech or a presentation? After all, there are many methods of communication: you could send an email, prepare a report, have a conference call, transmit a fax, write a book, or even spray-paint graffiti on a wall. With all of these options, just when is it appropriate to deliver a speech? What is unique about this form of communication that makes it the preferable means of communication for a given circumstance?

If your goal is help people absorb large amounts of data, you are better off providing copious well-written documents. Documents can be read, re-read, underlined, filed, and then pulled out again at will.

What if your goal is to entertain? It is far better to create a well-produced movie than to just give a speech.

So what, exactly, is a speech good for?

Inspiration.

Speeches are good for inspiring your audience, for getting them to understand your passion for a subject and hoping some of that passion rubs off on them in the process. Whenever I explain this, the first reaction I encounter is this:

"But TJ, I am a serious business person. It sounds like you are trying to turn me into some cheesy motivational speaker. What next, my own 800 number and a late night infomercial? Give me a break!"

I am NOT talking about inspiring or motivating in some generic and therefore useless sense of how to be richer, happier, and thinner through "positive thinking." Instead, I mean that good speakers "inspire" and "motivate" audience members to do such things as wear hard hats with a higher frequency, meet sales quotas, give better customer service, or clean-up trash in the office lunch room.

Facts are important, and numbers can be insightful, but never lose sight of the idea that your primary responsibility as a good speaker is to inspire. If you can't even get inspired to do this, then don't give a speech. Send an email instead.

The Common Leadership Trait

Political, business, and cultural leaders come in many sizes, shapes, styles, and skill levels. Some rise at 4:00a.m., some work from noon to 2:00 a.m.. Some are teetotalers, and some like to drink a fifth a day.

Leaders often become leaders because they are experts at motivating other people to do that which they would not normally want to do. Further, leaders learn how to delegate effectively. Corporate leaders delegate sales, advertising, and accounting, while political leaders delegate the planning and fighting of wars.

However, there is one thing that all real leaders know they can not delegate: speaking on behalf of their organization to the outside world. The President of the United States must be able to speak on behalf of the entire American public when addressing the country and the rest of the world. Likewise, a corporate CEO must be able to speak on behalf of the company to clients, customers, employees, vendors, analysts, investors, and the news media.

This cannot be delegated to staff.

Consequently, the most common trait among true leaders is the ability to communicate well, especially through the spoken word. Of course, speaking styles can vary among leaders, but at some point, most leaders find their own way of being an effective speaker.

There is more to being a leader than just speaking well. Wisdom, judgment, and principles are also essential. However, try to imagine a wise and principled Winston Churchill who was afraid to give a speech. Impossible! Churchill's wisdom, judgment, and principles would never have been applied to the world stage if he had not been able to communicate them via the spoken word.

More than height, appearance, wealth, or even charm, the ability to speak publicly is the one true "x" factor that creates a great leader. In fact, strong communication skills can prove to be invaluable when there is nothing else a leader can do but address the public in a certain situation.

Take for example the case of New York City Mayor Rudy Giuliani during the 9-11 crisis. By every traditional measure of leadership (i.e., making unpopular decisions, mobilizing the public to make sacrifices, and anticipating and preventing a danger to citizens), how did Giuliani fare?

I would contend that Giuliani didn't display any of the actions most commonly associated with great acts of political leadership in the realm of Lincoln or Churchill. I'm not criticizing Giuliani. I honestly don't think the mayor of any city could have been able to do much more than Giuliani did. In fact, I even voted for Giuliani in his re-election bid.

But why, in the aftermath of 9-11, was Giuliani hailed as a hero across the country and the world? What did Giuliani actually DO to achieve such universal acclaim?

He talked. He communicated. He expressed emotions. He spoke from the head and the heart without notes. For several weeks, Giuliani was the nation's talk show host-in-chief. He became an "Oprah-for-all" and was a ratings hit, especially since he was a more talented communicator than the New York Governor or President of the United States at the time.

So ingrained in people is the belief that outstanding communication skills are the hallmark of the great leader, that sometimes a single speech or series of public presentations is enough to burnish an image of heroic leadership.

The Four Corners

There are four goals you should try to accomplish every time you give a presentation:

1. Speak so that your audience understands you.
2. Speak so that your audience remembers your messages.
3. Motivate your audience to act on your message.
4. Motivate your audience to tell other people about your message.

1. People have to *UNDERSTAND* what you are saying.

The first goal of speaking so that people understand you is relatively easy. In fact, most people do speak in a way that is understandable. As long as you avoid excessive jargon and don't have a strong accent that is alien to your audience, chances are people will understand what you are saying.

2. Your audience needs to *REMEMBER* what you said.

The second goal of speaking so that people remember what you said is tough to accomplish. Really tough! Most speakers package their ideas in such a boring manner that the audience remembers nothing about the presentation five minutes after it has concluded. In truth, how many times have you personally sat through a conference filled with speaker after speaker for one or two days, and when it was all over, you couldn't associate any one new idea with a specific speaker? After all, there is a big difference in speaking in a way that is understandable versus speaking in a way that is both understandable and memorable.

3. Your audience must *ACT* on what you've asked them to do.

Unless you are a college professor or a humorist, you speak with the intent to motivate people to actually DO something, i.e., sign a contract, work harder, wear hard hats, or not sexually harass employees. The hard part is actually getting them to do these things based on your speech alone.

4. Your audience should *TELL OTHERS* what you said.

The real power in speaking is not just reaching the audience in the room or watching any one show. The strength comes from getting people who heard you to go to work for you at no cost by telling other people what you said. Think of it as multi-level marketing without the cheese and sleaze.

Most speakers accomplish only the first task when they are speaking (and sometimes not even that). Yes, the audience understood them, but that's it. The speaker was either so abstract or so boring that nobody remembers anything he said. Since nobody remembered anything, they certainly didn't act on whatever it was the speaker wanted them to do, and they sure as heck didn't tell other people anything about the speaker's message (other than that it was great for curing insomnia).

There is just one type of speaker who can be successful by only accomplishing the first of our four speaking requirements—the standup comedian. Granted, he has the additional and incredibly difficult task of trying to make us laugh every 12 seconds. However, a comedian can be very successful without the audience necessarily remembering any jokes, taking action, or telling other people the jokes they heard. Hearing comedy is about getting a laugh at that moment and nothing else.

If you give a clear, logical and rational presentation of facts but your audience remembers nothing, what did you accomplish? Bad standup comedy, and that's it. (I'm presuming your quarterly review of your department's budget objectives does not leave superiors doubled over with belly laughs.)

There is no reason to settle for being a bad standup comedian—ever!

By my estimation, 95 percent of all business speakers fall into the first category—the only thing they do is speak in an understandable way. They are not memorable; therefore, they create no change in anyone's behavior. In other words, the speech WAS A TOTAL WASTE OF TIME FOR EVERYONE INVOLVED.

When you think of a great speech like Martin Luther King, Jr.'s "I Have a Dream," it is easy to see how he accomplished all four presentation objectives. His audience understood his message, they remembered it, they acted upon it by demanding changes in laws, and they told other people about his message, thus galvanizing the whole civil rights movement.

Don't let yourself off the hook by thinking, "Hey, I'm not trying to save the world with my little presentation, all I have to do is decrease our injury rate on the job by 12 percent."

The goals of the speech are still the same, and even in this situation you need to get people to take action, no matter how small. Accomplishing all four objectives in a speech has nothing to do with the topic and everything to do with whether you care enough about your audience and your objectives to genuinely communicate in a captivating manner.

So, you have a choice in how you are going to make your presentation. You could stand up in front of workers and bore them with statistics and abstractions and tell them "management says we have to decrease injuries," or you could be more captivating. Perhaps drop an egg on the floor to symbolize what happens to your brain on the construction site if a metal beam falls on your head from 20 feet above and you have no hard hat on. Then, you could show a photo of a colleague who got hurt last year on the job site because he wasn't wearing a hard hat. Next, show a picture of his spouse who now has to work three jobs and come home to a husband who can't get out of bed. Finally, end your presentation by literally putting the hard hat on and asking everyone else in the room to do so too.

If you don't accomplish all four goals during a presentation, you haven't done yourself much good, and you've likely wasted your audience's time. So, always keep in mind your four speaking goals when you are writing or preparing your speech, when you are delivering it, and when you are receiving feedback from your audience after the speech.

It's Not About You

The biggest fundamental difference between average or decent speakers and great speakers is that exceptional speakers realize that the speech isn't about them, but it's about the audience.

If you are focused on yourself, you end up thinking about yourself to the point where you get nervous. If you are preoccupied with your audience members and their learning experience, you don't have time to get nervous!

Me-centered speakers play it safe because they are worried about saving face and remaining "respectable." Audience-centered speakers take risks because they know that the worst that can happen is their audience might not learn as much as they want them to learn, but in this instance, at least the monotony was broken.

Self-centered speakers put numerous words on their PowerPoint slides because it makes it easier for them to remember what to say, never mind that it is boring to the audience. The audience-centered speaker never puts words on a slide. Instead, he or she puts interesting and memorable images on slides. Further, the audience-centered speaker puts notes on a small note card that only he or she can see.

In contrast, the me-centered speaker wastes time at the beginning thanking the audience, talking about how happy he is to be there and explaining why and how he decided to talk about the topic and how he decided to organize the topic. The audience-centered speaker, from the very second she opens her mouth, says something of interest and relevance to the audience and never uses boring clichéd formalities.

The me-centered speaker can flawlessly execute a speech, use perfect diction, and still come across as a self-centered prig, while the audience-centered speaker can occasionally mispronounce a word, lose his place, or make a stumble, and still come across as sincere, powerful, and have an impact.

At the end of the speech, the self-centered speaker asks, "How'd I do? How many people applauded? How many people gave me a four star rating?"

The audience-centered speaker asks, "Did the audience learn as much as they could? What can I do to give the audience more value? Can I help the next audience learn even more?"

Are you going to focus on yourself or your audience? You might not know, but your audience will figure it out instantly.

The "X" Fun Factor

I am often asked, "What is the difference between a good communicator and a great communicator?"

In professional golf, the difference between someone who makes a fortune on the tour and someone who has to be his own caddy, on average, is only a couple of stroke. Similarly, with people who give speeches, the difference between the good and the great is very small.

In fact, the "good" presenters often make fewer mistakes, stumble less, or jump around less frequently. The "great" speakers often

make all these blunders and more, and yet they still come across as fantastic and memorable communicators.

Why?

The difference all comes down to fun. Fantastic communicators are having fun when they present. The fun shows in their face, eyes, voice, hands, and body language.

Great speakers consistently communicate the following:

"There is no place on earth I'd rather be than speaking in front of you right now."

This attitude permeates not only how the speaker communicates a message but also how the audience receives the message. Audiences respond very well to genuine passion in a speaker. Note that I am not saying that in order to be a good speaker you have to jump up and down like a TV preacher or sound full of hype like that kid on the infomercials selling a get-rich-quick scheme involving selling stuff through "tiny, tiny classified ads" (if only you will first send him $245).

There is no one model for a communicator to display the fact that he or she is having a lot of fun when talking about a subject. But, like Justice Potter Stewart who couldn't define pornography but knew it

when he saw it, both live and TV audiences instantly feel when a presenter is having fun. Audiences might not know why, but they feel it in their bones.

The next question I get is,

"TJ, how in the heck can I have fun when I'm nervous, and I'd rather be receiving heart surgery without anesthesia than giving a speech or appearing on TV?"

Sadly, I have no simple magic answer for you. Betty Buckley is a Broadway star in part because of daily practice for decades. Even the 14-year-old prodigies who occasionally spring up in women's tennis, golf, and ice-skating didn't become great overnight. They practiced for hours a day for a decade before they went pro.

Fortunately, you don't have to give presentations for hours a day to become great, but you do have to give them often enough so that you are no longer excessively nervous. Then, and only then, can you focus on the joy of communicating about your subject of choice.

Test, Test, Test

It never ceases to amaze me how so many hard-nosed businessmen and women demand proof for everything they do. They want proof to justify a new marketing program. They want a specific Return On Investment down to the penny before they begin a new advertising campaign. Yet, these very same executives continue investing their money, time, energy, and resources into giving speeches the same way for 50 years, without a shred of evidence that what they are doing is effective.

There is a lot of bad advice out there on how to give presentations, such as "Don't gesture with your hands." Therefore, I urge people to be highly skeptical of all speech-training gurus, myself included. However, this skepticism should be consistent in all aspects of presentation preparation and delivery.

I often introduce concepts to my presentation-training clients that appear to be radical, such as, "Don't put any words on PowerPoint slides; rather, use only images, photos, drawings or graphs." The reaction I get is often, "That's absurd! Everyone I know fills his PowerPoint slides with words, sentences, and whole paragraphs."

And I respond, "Don't take my word for it. Test it."

If you put a whole bunch of words on a slide and read from it during a presentation, where is your proof that this is effective in

communicating your message? Sure, other people do it that way, but where is your proof?

Test your PowerPoint slides. It's not a hard thing to do. Simply find five colleagues on their lunch hour and practice your PowerPoint slide presentation in front of them. Don't tell them in advance that you will be testing them. After your presentation, ask them to describe all of the slides they remember and the points they represent. If no one in your test audience can remember certain slides (or most of them), then delete the slides. The slides are there to help your audience understand and remember your key points. If they don't do that, then get rid of them. You cannot hurt your presentation by deleting your slides because you have already proven they are ineffective.

Let's say you add a bunch of glitzy video with thumping rock music to your presentation. Why not when others in your industry do? But, where is the proof that the video will actually improve your audience's understanding of your message? Again, trot out five colleagues at lunchtime and have them watch your whole presentation, video included. Then, test them on their comprehension. If the video doesn't get the job done, then get rid of it.

You may like to start off your speech by thanking everyone, telling them you are pleased to be there and that you are going to talk about

W, X, Y, and Z today. After all, that's how most people begin presentations. But, where is your proof that this is the most effective way to begin a presentation? Test it in front of a sample audience. What you may find is that your opening is nothing more than a good way to convince people that you can speak a bunch of meaningless clichés.

Many complex new technologies and products can be very difficult to test without first spending a fortune on research and development. Fortunately, a new speech is not as complicated. You can test your presentations cheaply, easily, and effectively. All you have to do is test your content and style in front of a few real people and then ask them what they remember. If they don't remember all of the key points that were really important for you to get across, then you can be 100 percent certain that your speech is ineffective, and you need to do a complete overhaul.

Moreover, chances are, the vast majority of what you think is fine in your speech isn't working. So, just keep what does work, and come up with new material and approaches until your presentation passes the test.

Chapter 1:
Speech Writing 101

Chapter 1:
Speech Writing 101

Nothing is Worse Than A
Well-Written Speech

"How is your speech going?"

"Great, I've just written my third draft. It's really shaping up nicely."

Danger! If you hear someone say this, you are usually in trouble if you are an audience member. Speeches that "read" well because they are "well written" are usually an unmitigated disaster for the audience.

Why?

Each medium is unique. The spoken word medium is entirely different from the written medium. That's why great actors usually don't make excellent singers or vice versa.

People hear differently than they read, and unless you grasp this fact, you will always write a bad speech.

When you are writing for the eye, you need to avoid repetition, vary the length of sentences, which includes having some long sentences,

and build on your ideas in a complex manner. Additionally, when you are writing, you need to use complete sentences. All of these traits will sink an actual speech delivered to a live audience.

Good speeches mimic great conversations. And when real people speak, they use incomplete sentences, lots of repetition, and generally short sentences. Most important, they use lots of real examples, personal stories, and dialogue.

If you actually write a speech well, one intended for the ear, it would look awful to the eye. So, if you craft a great presentation for your boss, chances are, when he reads it, he will think you are a complete illiterate!

Consequently, what do most corporate and political speech writers do? They play it safe to avoid the wrath of their boss's critical reading eye. The speechwriters prepare a speech that will withstand the eye of reading editors. The focus is no longer on the real customer—the audience member listening to the speaker.

If you are going to write a speech, keep these guidelines in mind:
- Avoid the word "which." This word makes sentences grow long and complex.
- Avoid references to "former" and "latter." These work in print, but just get people lost when they are listening to you.

- Always use contractions. Nothing shouts out awkward, poorly written speech like the failure to use contractions.
- Watch out for sibilants. Too many S's in a row cause big problems, especially if you are around a microphone.
- Don't use the third person; it sounds stilted and too formal. Use "I, me, and you." Don't say "one does not do that."

Many words and phrases look good on paper but sound awkward when you actually try to say them. The most important tip to follow with written speeches is to speak them out into an audio or video recorder several times before you deliver it to the real audience. Listen carefully to how the speech sounds after each rehearsal. Be harshly critical of your own speech. If any word or phrase sounds awkward, re-work it or get rid of it.

Spell It Out

When you are speaking to colleagues and other peers within your industry, the tendency is to use lots of acronyms and initials, instead of speaking out the entire word or phrase. This saves time and makes you seem like a knowledgeable insider, right?

Wrong!

Other than IRS, FBI, or NFL, you should shun using initials and acronyms when you are speaking. Here's why:

1. Most of your audience may understand you, but 10 percent may be new to your industry, and they will have no idea what you are talking about.

2. Many in your audience may be familiar with insider lingo because they read it in professional literature frequently, but they don't "hear" the lingo spoken. Therefore, they need a second to process and translate your lingo. They do get it, but they are now a second behind in your speech and are missing other elements of your content.

3. By speaking out all of the words rather than the initials, you slow down the amount of content you are putting out. This

is a good thing because it makes it easier for audience members to follow what you are saying.

4. Knowledgeable audience members who know what all the initials stand for will rarely be offended if you spell out the words.

5. Audience members who don't know what your acronyms stand for will use this as an excuse to tune out your speech, and once you have lost them, it's nearly impossible to bring their attention back to what you are saying.

6. Some people in the audience will be judging your long-term leadership capabilities. If you speak with nothing but jargon and acronyms, they will judge you as someone who is not capable of future assignments that might require you to speak to larger audiences comprised of non-insiders. This can destroy your chances of promotion without you ever realizing it.

7. There is something aesthetically less than pleasing about the sight of someone spouting off lots of initials and acronyms, even if everyone understands the speaker. If you don't use as many buzzwords or initials, you won't seem like a pinhead. Besides, it doesn't take that much longer to say

"Client Wallet Emptying Process" than it does to say "CWEP."

If you still can't seem to rid yourself of the habit of using insider jargon, initials, and acronyms, there is at least one major compromise you can and should make. Say out the entire phrase the first time you use it in the speech. After that, you may use just the initials. That way, you at least bring some members of your audience in from the dark and create a better reputation for yourself in the process.

The Speaker's Enemy-Abstraction

The number one enemy of the public speaker is abstraction. Think of your speech in comparison to describing a forest to your audience: Many speakers get greedy and try to paint a picture of a 30,000-foot high view of the whole forest with their words. It is far better to paint the picture of one unique tree in vivid and unforgettable detail than to only give an abstract view of yet another forest.

Boring speakers speak at only one level during their entire presentation—30,000 feet. Successful speakers are constantly changing their levels of abstraction. They may start off by introducing a concept at a very high altitude, and then they come

down a notch by giving examples. Next, they may lower altitude again with a few more facts. Finally, they tell a story fleshing out their abstract concept by using real people, places, emotions and actions that the audience member can see, feel, and almost touch (equal to the vivid details of one tree).

Stories, facts, and examples drive the abstract point home so that it is remembered. Only after this has been accomplished should you move on to the next abstract point. If it takes five minutes to get from one abstract point to the next, so be it. The skilled speaker knows that no one is going to remember 197 abstract concepts and facts presented in a straightforward linear manner; therefore, why bother?

The human brain is not wired to remember abstract facts that it hears only once. Our brains need more stimulation. Our memories are triggered much more by the visual than they are by sound. This is why successful speakers tell stories that their audiences can visualize.

When I am asked to introduce myself to a new group of media training clients, I don't just tell them I have "media experience." That is abstract and unmemorable. Instead, I tell them a story about the time a talk show host in a South Florida radio station pulled a gun on me during a live interview and how I managed to get out of there alive. Those are images that audiences can visualize and

remember—and it drives the point home that I have been in a variety of tough media situations, plus it is a true story.

The skilled speaker is constantly changing the level of abstraction when he or she speaks. If you were charting his or her course, it would look like someone constantly running up and down a staircase. At the top, they introduce one abstraction. At the bottom, they tell a real life story. Anyone can tell a story from the bottom, and anyone can introduce abstracts from the top, but the memorable speaker will be constantly running up and down the staircase.

Constant change. Variety. Abstract examples, examples, examples. Abstract examples, examples. That's what will engage your audience.

More Magical Than
Please Or Thank You

For the public speaker, there is no phrase more magical than "For example…." It is extraordinarily difficult to overuse the phrase and extremely common to under-use it.

The magic in the phrase is that it forces the speaker to get his or her head out of the clouds and come down to the ground. This is not to suggest that your audience is comprised of simpletons incapable of

abstract thought. It's just that your audience, like all audiences, does not absorb abstract thoughts when hearing them or reading them.

"For example…" forces you the speaker to bring to life the principle or concept you articulated moments ago. If someone in your audience didn't understand your concept, your example might now make it understandable. Further, if someone else in your audience did understand your concept, your example might make it much more memorable.

Finally, another audience member might be so enthusiastic about your concept that your example now gives that person a shorthand way of explaining it to other people.

As a speaker, finding examples is a good exercise for you to sharpen your thinking and to test the relevance of your concepts for a particular audience. If no examples pop in your mind when going through your message points, it may be a good indication that you have the wrong messages.

Skilled communicators consistently alternate between abstract thought and concrete thought. By using examples liberally, you are forcing yourself to abandon abstract thought as you describe someone, something, or some case study in concrete terms.

Lazy, ineffective communicators routinely shun examples and all concrete case studies. They erroneously think that they don't have time for such foolishness, or that their audiences will find examples condescending. Moreover, bad communicators are universally infected with the belief that since they have hundreds upon hundreds of brilliant ideas to share with an audience, they need to proceed as quickly as possible, leaving no time to provide examples.

So, when it comes to facts and concepts in a speech, more is not more; rather, more is less. To the contrary, when it comes to giving examples, more really is more.

Don't Think On Your Feet, Think On Your Seat

My clients often tell me before we begin a training session that they want to learn how to better "think on their feet" during presentations and question and answer sessions.

My response is, "Why?"

The skill of thinking on one's feet is highly overrated. It is far better to actually develop the discipline of preparing in advance and rehearsing. Of course, this is hard work., but if you consistently

think about your message and all of the issues surrounding your topic, you will rarely be surprised.

So, if you want to appear to be good at thinking on your feet, spend some time thinking on your seat in front of your computer writing down notes, outlines, bullet points, and sample questions and answers. Then, you can make it all look easy.

Never, Ever, Ever, Ever Apologize

Um, hi. I was planning on writing a great chapter here, but, um, well, you see, I just got a new upgrade on my Windows operating system this morning, and I haven't figured out how to use all of the new elements of my MS Word program. I meant to learn my new system earlier last week, but I had to fly to Wahington, DC, and then stay an extra day, so things have been in a real rush this week. Aslo, Im afrid I havent learnd how to use my new speel check function, so youll half to bare with me. Will you accept my apologiesz?

No, chances are you would not accept my apologies if I were to give you a written document that begins like the above paragraph. In fact, I'm lucky if you are still reading.

You would never dream of sending an important document to a client or even a simple email to a colleague that was written similar to the paragraph above. It would be too embarrassing. Plus, you would know instinctively that nobody else really cares whether or not you understand your word processor. They just want to get your message quickly and clearly from reading your text.

Unfortunately, though, the paragraph is a true example of the way many people start important speeches to large groups of customers, clients, colleagues, and industry representatives.

Why do people do this?

They complain that they didn't have time to rehearse their PowerPoint or that their video wasn't working with their other software or their staff didn't prepare the right material— everything but the dog ate their speech. It's embarrassing, and yet, it happens all the time.

Before you make such an egregious blunder, stop and realize one thing: Your audience doesn't give a darn about you. They don't care about the process you went through to create your presentation. They just want the results of it.

When people sit down to listen to you speak, they are thinking primarily one thing, "How can I learn something here that is going to help make my life more productive, easier, or more interesting?"

Your audience is focused on itself—and that is exactly where you should be focused too. If my keyboard jams in the process of writing this chapter, you expect me to stop, go buy another keyboard, install it properly, and keep writing, all without ever telling you a single boring detail regarding my computer problems. It is the same for presenting. Your audience expects you to do your homework before you get up to speak.

So, if you apologize for not being well-prepared for your speech, what the audience really hears you say is this, "You people are so unimportant to me that I think one hour of my time is more important than the collective 100 hours of your time. That's why I didn't bother practicing, and that's why I'm going to bore you now."

If your PowerPoint slides are not in the right order, that's not the audience's fault. If this happens, your audience will be thinking, "Either take the time to get it right, or don't bother agreeing to give a presentation in the first place."

Therefore, please remember that apologizing, at the beginning or at any other time, during a speech is never acceptable or helpful. If you

have given your audience at least the minimum respect it deserves, your apologies will never be needed. And, if you do make some mistake, don't feel the need to draw attention to it by apologizing, simply correct yourself and continue in a nonchalant manner.

A Few Notes On Notes

Anytime you see a fawning profile of a politician on the rise you invariably see a clause somewhere in the story that says, "And Senator Smithers is such a natural on the stump that he can speak for an hour without using notes."

What's going on here? Why is it bad to use notes?

Actually, it is no sin to use notes while speaking; instead, it all depends on how you use them. As I have stressed before, it is deadly dull to use PowerPoint slides as your notes because everyone else can see them. Your notes are just for you.

"But TJ, how will I know what PowerPoint slide is next if I don't have all of my notes on the slides?" Simply put your notes on a piece of paper.

Ultimately, your audience rates you subconsciously on your relationship with your notes. If you are holding onto your notes for

dear life, reading from them, and flipping through the pages, your audience will penalize you in their assessment of your speaking skills. If, however, you refer to your notes in a subtle, indirect, and undetectable manner, your audience will be highly impressed.

Ronald Reagan always spoke from note cards, but you never saw him holding them up, fumbling with them, or flipping them. How did he do this?

Reagan would stride to the lectern with his hands free. Once he was at the lectern, he would look up and out at his audience. He would smile and wink at certain audience members. Then, and only then, would he reach down with his left hand into his left suit jacket pocket and pull out a stack of note cards. Notice that he never pulled them out of his inside top pocket—that would have been too noticeable. Only after delivering his first line while looking up at his audience did he even dare to look down at his notes for the first time. By then, he had already established a professional and commanding presence with his audience. He never picked up his notes in front of his audience, and he never played with them. He kept them out of sight, and so should you.

The most effective way to use notes is to use a series of one, two, or three word phrases that will remind you of your key messages and points for each PowerPoint slide. You can use 3x5 cards, 4x6 cards or regular 8 ½ x 11 sheets of paper. My own preference is to tear an

8 ½ x 11 sheet of paper into two, so that it is now 4 ½ by 11. I then use the paper to write words in a column format.

When using your notes while giving your PowerPoint slides, the key is diverting your audience so they can't see you peeking at your notes. When I give my standard eight-hour presentation training course to a group of executives, I start the day with a 75 minute PowerPoint presentation on how to use PowerPoint effectively. I use more than 40 slides during the presentation. I always introduce the slide before it is shown and can talk about it vividly right before I flash it all on the screen.

Is this because I was blessed with a superhuman memory capable of remembering 75 minutes worth of material and the exact sequence of 40 slides?

No way. I am just sneakier than most speakers.

I have a word or short phrase that tells me what each slide is about typed on my 4 ½ x 11 sheet of paper already sitting on my laptop. The paper is already sitting on the laptop before the presentation/training starts. I never refer to my notes during the first five minutes because I don't refer to any slides the first five minutes. When the time comes to show the first slide, I don't have to look at my notes because even I can remember my first slide.

Here is where the real trick comes in. When I take a half-second to bend over the computer to hit "enter" to bring up the next slide, I am also looking at my notes to see what the slide after that will be. My audience thinks I am just hitting enter. They have no idea I am looking at notes.

I never have to waste time worrying about what slide comes next or mixing up the order. Everything is right in front of me, and I can look at all of my notes regularly. It's just that my audience never sees me stopping the action unnaturally to look at my notes. The audience is expecting a one or two second pause when you bend down to hit the key to advance the frame or even if you are using a remote control. So, use that second to your advantage.

There is another opportunity for looking at your notes without detection. At the exact moment when you have flashed a new PowerPoint Image up on a screen and turn to it and point, all heads in your audience will then be staring directly at your screen. Now you can glance at your notes, and no one will ever notice.

The first thing you can do to get dramatically better with your use of notes is to force yourself to use no more than one page. If you can't get your notes down to one page, perhaps you need to ask yourself how interesting your material is if you can't even remember it without having to have numerous pages of notes.

Once you get it down to one page of notes, many other problems disappear magically. You don't have to worry about turning or shuffling pages or getting them out of order. Because it is one page, you should never have to touch your notes. Also, make sure they are typed in a font large enough for you to see without having to hold them close to your eyes. As mentioned above, if you are manually hitting your keyboard, the best place for your notes is on the left side of your keyboard. If you are not pushing the keyboard, then you may want to put your notes on a flat table. If you are in front of a large audience on a stage, you can have a small table with a glass of water on it. Have your notes placed there in advance and you can glance down as you walk by or stop, seemingly just to pick up a glass of water.

If there is a lectern nearby, you can use that for your notes. However, don't use it the way most speakers do—with the notes in the middle forcing you to stand directly behind it. Instead, place your notes on one side of the lectern at an angle. That way you can glance at your notes when you are not behind the lectern. This way, it will appear as though you are just walking by the lectern with your head down, spontaneously thinking up a new idea.

Again, your audience will never know you are looking at your notes.

Unless you are a Broadway actor, there is no reason you should have to memorize all of your words for a PowerPoint presentation. Use notes, but use them without being noticed, and you will receive the maximum credit from your audience.

Notes To Your Demise

On Donald Trump's show The Apprentice, one of the apprentices, Troy, was making the case on why he should not be fired. Troy wanted to make his case in a logical manner and had, thus, written down notes, to which he was now referring.

Trump forcefully interjected, "Stop reading your notes! Just talk to me."

The startled aspiring apprentice quickly did as he was told, but his fate was now sealed—he was fired within moments of committing the communications blunder.

Was Trump correct in being offended by his underling using notes in a meeting? In this case I would rate Donald's ability to assess strong communication ahead of his taste in hairdressers or interior design.

Trump instinctively knows that during intense and emotional communication moments, such as when you are pleading with your boss not to end your career, it is simply not effective to be seen as reading from notes. Reading is primarily an intellectual activity, whereas begging to avoid the death penalty is an emotional activity. There are times when communicating is about expressing your passion, conviction, sincerity, and commitment. The act of reading or even glancing at notes works against all of these communication goals.

Trump was following the old adage "never trust a man who won't look you in the eye." You can't look someone in the eye if you are reading notes.

The lesson here is that notes should never be used during times of highly intense communication where you are covering emotional and personal topics. You wouldn't want to refer to notes when telling your spouse you want a divorce. Likewise, notes won't fly when you are asking for a raise from your boss. It's fine to use notes in a presentation when you are giving specific numbers for next year's sales quotas, but when you are trying to motivate employees to work harder, longer, and smarter, you had better look at them right in their eye, and make sure the notes are hidden.

Otherwise, your audience will fire you, without even telling you.

Never read a speech to your audience. Never read a speech. NEVER READ A SPEECH!

I say that all the time to my clients. Every presentation coach makes this statement. Why?

Because 99.99999 percent of the world reads a speech in such a way that their voice becomes flat, monotone, lifeless, and boring. The audience falls instantly to sleep.

However, there is a way to read a speech effectively, even though the method is rarely used. Ronald Reagan was a practitioner of this art form, and I'm not talking about when he or others use a TelePrompTer.

Here is the process. You reformat your speech on your page so that there is only one phrase per line (not a whole sentence, just one phrase). The phrase must be short enough that it fits on one line and does not have to continue onto the next line.

Next, you leave a space between each line of text.

Now comes the reading part, and this is the hard part. You must silently look down at your paper and read a line, then look up and give someone in your audience direct eye contact. Then, and only then, do you verbalize the line. You must say it in a conversational

way, full of inflection. It doesn't have to be memorized because it is very short, and you just read it a second ago. If you change a word here or there, it shouldn't matter. The key is to say it so that you sound like you are just talking to one person in an informal way.

The next part is tricky for most people. You must pause, silently, while you glance back down at your notes to read the next line. Your audience will appreciate the pause, as it gives them a chance to catch up and digest what you are saying. Your pauses will make you seem much more confident and relaxed.

The problem for most speakers is that it feels awkward and weird to pause while they are reading the next line. So, what do they do? They figure, "I'll kill two birds with one stone and read and talk at the same time." This puts us back to the beginning: sounding flat, boring, and monotone.

The key is to never read when you are talking and never talk when you are reading. If you can just master the concept of doing one thing at a time, you can effectively read a speech to any audience.

Words Are Not What's Most Important

Many people scoff at the early 1970's UCLA study that found only 7 percent of the impression a speaker leaves on an audience comes from the words he or she uses. The study claims that 55 percent comes from body language and movement and 38 percent from how the voice is used.

This seems absurd to many people. That's why 99 percent of corporate America spends 99 percent of its time focusing on the words that go into a presentation. While I have told my clients for many years about this breakdown of impact among the voice, words, and body movement, even I have had my doubts about the preciseness of the findings. 7 percent just seems too low of an impact for words.

However, after recently conducting speech training for a leader of a foreign government, I gained a new understanding for this 5538-7 percent rule. This foreign leader was giving a speech in a language that I didn't know. I videotaped the speech, as I do in all training sessions. Then, we played it back and critiqued it together (the foreign leader did speak English too, lucky for me).

I pointed out that his hands weren't moving, and he seemed stiff. He agreed. I told him that although I didn't know what he was saying, I did know that he sounded too monotone and he was putting me to

sleep. He confessed that it sounded boring to him as well. Then, I pointed out that his volume and energy level was much lower than his normal speaking voice. Again, he pled guilty. Finally, I pointed out how his eyes were darting around at me and other people in the room, and I felt like he wasn't really focused on anyone. He noticed this as well.

He did the speech three more times, each followed by critiques. By the end, he and his advisors thought he had improved dramatically. Instead of committing malpractice, my inability to understand his language was only a small liability.

The real lesson is that if you are boring, you will be able to bore people no matter what language they speak. If you are captivating, you will be able to engage people, even if they have no idea what you are saying. Of course, content is important—you must have good words to share, but you must convey it with your body and your voice to be convincing to your audience.

Chapter 2:
The Art Of Presenting

Chapter 2:
The Art Of Presenting

Break Out The Tux And Gown

If there is one misconception I wish I could eliminate, it would be the notion of a "formal speech."

There is no such thing as a "formal speech." There is no such thing as an "informal speech." There are only two types of presentations in the world:

1. Interesting speeches that are memorable, and
2. Boring speeches that are forgettable.

That's it!

The second I hear clients tell me they are about to give a "formal speech" and they want to rehearse, I put the coffeepot on overdrive, and I cool our training studio down to 65 degrees. I immediately know I am about to be subjected to a snooze fest, and it will be a struggle to stay awake.

Of course you may find yourself in presentation situations that are more structured than others. This occurs when you are given exactly 20 minutes to make a new business pitch to an important prospective client, and they are seeing five of your competitors

before you and another 10 after. There may even be times when the entire future of your company is at stake, and you have exactly 15 minutes to speak to 500 people at an investor conference.

So yes, there are some speaking opportunities that have higher stakes or are just more structured than others. Yet, the problem is that most speakers think that a so-called formal speech is an excuse to throw-out their natural strengths as communicators.

To most business communicators, a formal speech means you do the following: stand stiff and rigid behind a lectern, quickly go through as many bullet-pointed facts and concepts as possible, use big words in long sentences, avoid contractions, eliminate examples and anecdotes, stop gesturing in a normal manner, and make your voice more monotone. And, to top it all off, in case there is anyone left who hasn't fallen asleep during the first five minutes of your speech, you read the rest of your speech with your head buried in your notes. If you were any more formal, you could be an extra on *Six Feet Under* as a cadaver.

Think about yourself when you are an audience member. Do you really think about whether you are listening to a formal speech or an informal speech? Of course not.

You are either thinking something like this: "This guy is boring me to tears. What a waste of time! Perhaps I'll pretend to take notes on my Palm so that I can actually check my email."

Or, you are thinking this: "This is interesting. I can see how this benefits me. I better make a note of this."

Those are the two main reactions to any speech.

So, the next time you have to give a so-called formal speech, remember that you still have the same responsibilities you have in any other speech. In addition to these four specific goals, all speakers should appear comfortable, confident, relaxed, and authoritative to their audiences.

Your style and substance are equally important in these speaking situations. That way, the only starch your audience members will observe is in your shirt, not your delivery.

Do Clothes Make The Person?

Style versus substance is the debate I face with many of my speech and media training clients. They think that media and presentation coaches want to focus purely on style, whereas the clients think of themselves as purists who are solely interested in substance.

This is a phony debate.

Anyone who wishes to maximize the impact of his or her substance will always spend a great deal of time, money, and effort on style as well. The two are as intertwined as stands of a thick rope.

George Washington was quite exacting in his white hosiery—he always had a regal look even though he turned down being named king of America. When approaching a city, he would get out of his coach and would ride in on white horse back. His image was crucial to his mission.

Winston Churchill gave much attention to the wide wale of his pinstripe, the bigness of his glasses, and the affectation of his cigar. Yes, he had substance, but he always extended it with style.

Do you ever remember seeing a single hair out of place on Margaret Thatcher's head? Of course not. That would have sullied her resolute, strong, principled political image.

Ronald Reagan would often joke about his age, but he knew this would only work if he appeared to be vital and healthy. Throughout his eight years in the White House, he never missed a secret Tuesday morning session with his hairdresser who magically preserved Reagan's head the color of chocolate ice cream.

Your style must complement and extend your message if you want to be effective. One reason Left-wing best selling writer and movie maker Michael Moore is successful is that his image is totally consistent with his message. He always wears a baseball cap, has exactly three and a half days of stubble on his face, and wears old t-shirts and jeans. For Moore and his "everyman" message, his "style" is perfect. To give Moore a haircut, close shave, and an Armani suite would rob him of his power just as surely as cutting Sampson's hair.

The key is to figure out your own substance or message and then come up with a style that communicates that message on its own.

Style is the best marketer substance ever had, and powerful leaders know this and embrace it—they don't whine and show disdain for mundane acts of image building.

What Do I Do With My Hands?

Several times each week, I have speech training clients who come into my training studio and express themselves in extraordinarily passionate, confident manners. Everything about their voice, body, and hand gestures conveys confidence.

Then, I put the video camera on them to practice a speech. Instantly, it's as if their arms became lifeless appendages that were sewn on to their torsos in the middle of the night—as devoid of nerve endings as a Punch-'N-Judy Doll. They sound and move like Zombies, and if their hands have any motion at all, it is to assume the military at-ease position or a fig-leaf position.

Inevitably, the client says to me, "What do I do with my hands? I never know what to do with my hands when I'm speaking."

So, what should you do with your hands when you are speaking?

This is the subject of a lot of misinformation. Someone somewhere told speakers that they should not gesture with their hands; because they will seem unprofessional, and somehow, this myth caught on.

Unfortunately, this is the worst advice any speaker has ever received.

Confident, comfortable people always gesture with their hands while speaking. Nervous people rarely ever move their hands. If you want to appear to be confident and comfortable, you should move your hands.

When you stop moving your hands, your body is moving less, so there is less variety of movements for people to see. Hence, you create a more boring visual experience for people watching you.

Yet, the fundamental reason you should move your hands when you speak to audiences is this: it is what you normally do when you are speaking to one person at a time. In fact, most people are hardwired to speak with their hands every time they open their mouth.

Susan Goldin-Meadow, author of *Hearing Gesture-How Our Hands Help Us Think*, shows clinical studies that reveal that even deaf, blind infants have to gesture when they are making sounds. Moving our hands when we make sounds from our mouth is how human beings are programmed!

For so many presenters, their nerves keep them from gesturing when they are in front of an audience, and this is the beginning of a process that destroys their entire presentation. By freezing their hands from their natural movements, they are tensing up their entire arms. This tension transfers to the rest of their body until, ultimately, it hits their vocal chords.

The result?

A voice that used to sound rich, energetic, and conversational, now sounds dull, flat, monotone, tense, lacking in energy, and low in volume.

The speech, at this point, is destined for failure. And it all started as a chain reaction from the speaker not using hand gestures in the way he or she normally does in everyday conversation.

The key is that it must feel natural to you. Don't consciously try to jab one finger or clench your fist with the thumb on top. Don't intentionally gesture with one hand while the other is in your pocket. Instead, use your hands the way you normally do.

Don't think you normally gesture with your hands?

You are wrong.

Most of my clients think they don't gesture with their hands. All I have to do is videotape them after they are through speaking a formal speech when they don't realize they are being taped. Once they tell me that they don't normally gesture much, I simply fast forward to the part of the tape when they didn't know they were being recorded. Inevitably they are gesturing a great deal, and in

turn, moving their arms, body, and head and sounding 1,000 times better than their formal speech a few minutes ago.

That always settles that argument. Use your hands.

Posture Is Paramount

When you get up to speak before a live audience, or if you are already standing and moving toward the front of the room to speak, all eyes are on you—and your posture. Your audience is instantly forming opinions about you, your confidence, your enthusiasm, and how interesting you will be. A great deal of this is based on how you are standing.

Many of us are nervous or shy when we have just been introduced, so without realizing it, we shrink ourselves by looking down, curling our shoulders down, and compressing our bodies. At a subconscious level, we are thinking, "If I make myself small enough, nobody will notice if I screw up."

This is the exact opposite of what you want to do.

Instead, you want to stand as tall as possible, without appearing to be stiff. It may be helpful to think of it as though you were trying to get the top of your head to touch an imaginary ceiling that is three

inches above you, while I'm not suggesting you get on your tiptoes or that you grimace trying to contort your body upward. Think of yourself as actually growing another couple of inches as you are walking up to speak (this will help your confidence too).

By holding yourself high, it is nearly impossible for your chest to cave inward in the manner that self-conscious people often do, which will prevent you from appearing to be slouching, leaning, or slumping in a sloppy fashion. Also, if you are holding yourself as high as possible, your stomach muscles will be working to lengthen your body, and you will benefit from a mild slimming effect.

However, one word of caution, if you try to hold yourself high and you stop moving your neck, head, body, or arms in a natural way, you will create an entirely counterproductive effect: you will seem like the Wizard of Oz's "Tin Man" (only dorkier).

So, before and during your presentation, hold yourself high, but remain fluid and natural.

Do You Need Training Wheels?

Lecterns are the training wheels of the speaking world. No self-respecting speaker would ever stand behind one. (Note: what most people call a podium is actually a lectern. A podium is the platform that a speaker stands on. A lectern is what a speaker stands behind and often puts notes on.)

There are several problems with using a lectern, including:

One, they rob a speaker of the ability to communicate with body language. The vast majority of the impression you leave with an audience comes not from your words but from your body language and sound. When you stand behind a lectern, you are hiding 75 percent of your body.

Two, speakers standing behind a lectern tend to grab it and hold it as they speak. Once you do this, you stop gesturing in a normal way. As mentioned earlier, if you stop gesturing normally, you look stiffer, less comfortable, and your voice will become flatter and more monotone.

Three, lecterns make it too easy to bury your head in your notes, thus losing eye contact with your audience.

Four, lecterns are often setup too far away from the first row of your audience, thus creating more distance and an unnecessary need for microphones. Further, if you are in a room speaking to 15 people, you don't need a microphone, but if you are at a lectern that puts you 30 feet away from them, then you likely do need the microphone.

Five, lecterns make the speaker seem like a coward who is afraid of the audience. It's almost like you fear the crowd will start throwing rotten vegetables at you during your presentation, and you need something to hide behind.

Six, lecterns limit your foot movement. If you can't move, you become a potted plant. This forces you to keep your distance from your audience, not just physically, but also emotionally.

Try to imagine Oprah hosting her talk show from behind a lectern, planted in one spot, with no hand gestures, eye contact, or other natural movements. Impossible!

"But TJ, the last five speakers all stood up and used the lectern, so I have to, right?"

"Wrong!"

When you are speaking, your only obligation is to communicate in the most effective manner to your audience. But, please notice that I said that no self-respecting speaker would stand BEHIND a lectern. I didn't say he or she wouldn't USE a lectern from time to time. As discussed before, there is nothing wrong with putting a single sheet of paper with large bullet point notes on top of a lectern. The skillful speaker will then walk near or next to the lectern from time to time to take a quick peek at their notes.

"But TJ, the microphone is attached to the lectern. I have to use the microphone or people won't hear me; therefore, I have to stand behind the lectern, right?"

Wrong again. Most microphones attached to lecterns can be bent a couple of feet in any direction. Simply bend the microphone away from the lectern and to one of the sides. Now you can stand next to the lectern and use the microphone without being obscured by the lectern. (But you should always request a wireless microphone in advance so that you won't be immobilized by a stationary mic.)

Set yourself free! Get rid of the lectern. You will come across infinitely more confidant, comfortable, and interesting.

Reading Ain't So Easy

We all learned to read in first grade, right? Well, it's not so easy in front of a crowd. But, there may be times when you have to read short snippets or a paragraph or two in front of people. Appropriate items could include a letter from someone important to your audience or a brief selection from a book you wrote. You might also want to read a selection of a memo you wrote to staff to give specific words even more importance or gravity.

When you interrupt a normal, well delivered, conversational, non-read speech with a brief reading selection, it can have a nice dramatic affect to your overall presentation—if you carry it off well. When reading a 10 to 30 second piece from a letter or your own writings, you do not have to pretend to be putting on an act. You are reading, and you aren't trying to fool anyone—and that's OK.

For a brief moment, the audience is paying slightly less attention to you and even more attention to the words. That's fine, as long as you get the words right. However, most presenters find that it is much more difficult to read aloud in front of an audience than it is to read silently.

Speakers often trip on words when reading aloud, lose their place, have to start over, or flub the most important point. Now, the

audience loses focus on the words and shifts its focus to you and the fact that you are appearing to be incompetent.

"How hard can it be to read a simple piece of paper?" your audience is wondering. Several things are happening here:

One, you might have "practiced" it by reading it silently and thinking about what you are going to say. This isn't really practicing in a helpful way. You must talk out your presentation, even any brief segments you plan on reading.

Two, you try to read from the original letter, memo, document, or book. This doesn't work because the font size is too small. It is easier on the eye if you reformat the material so that it is double or triple the normal font size.

Three, your lighting at the lectern might be much weaker than normal reading light, making it hard to see the words clearly.

Four, nervousness comes to most of us when we are speaking in front of people, and the larger the crowd, the more nervous most people get. Sadly, that nervousness drains our brains of their normal skills. Suddenly, even something as simple as reading becomes difficult and laborious.

Fifth, you can't find your reading glasses!

Don't make the mistake of assuming that a portion of your presentation that is to be read will be easier or take less preparation time than the rest of your speech.

Practice, rehearse, get a bigger font, then practice more. This is the only way to come across naturally as though you are casually picking up something to read and share with your audience.

You Are What You Drink

Although you should drink plenty of water before you go on TV, heed this advice: "Too much of a good thing isn't a good thing."

I once quickly drank a 32-ounce Big Gulp Coke before a four-hour, talk-radio hosting gig. All of the sudden I got the hiccups. And I don't mean a small case of barely noticeable hiccups. These were violent, chest-cavity spasms that practically knocked me out of my chair every 20 seconds.

To make matters worse, I had no guests for the final two hours of the program and darn few callers. So bathroom breaks were few! Still worse, the hiccups were so ridiculous that I couldn't stop laughing after each episode. Never a good combination – laughter and a full bladder. Fortunately for me, this did not take place during a ratings-sweep week. Don't let this happen to you.

A note on carbonated beverages in general. When you are speaking, you are using your vocal cords. It is your job to protect them, nurture them and make them feel comfortable before you speak so that they won't fail you when you need them. (Although unrelated to protecting your voice, carbonated beverages can also make you hiccup and belch – never attractive in any human encounter – and when consumed in excess, they make you have to use the bathroom.)

Drinking coffee may seem like a good idea, especially before speaking at a breakfast meeting or an early morning talk-radio show. But the caffeine can make you jittery and even more nervous. Starbucks will hate me for this, but even the decafs can be problematic if you put milk in your drink. Milk creates extra mucus in the mouth, which makes it harder to talk clearly. You could also burn your tongue or another body part easily, which would really make for an unpleasant interview. So skip the coffee and avoid milk or anything with milk in it.

Alcohol?

You've got to be kidding. I know many people who claim to have done a shot or two to calm their nerves, especially before speaking at an evening meeting. And yes, some singers use beer to "loosen" their vocal cords, but this is a bad idea for several reasons:

- Alcohol affects the memory, so you are more likely to have your mind go blank in the middle of a speech.
- Alcohol is more likely to make you sweat, which doesn't make a good impression on your audience.
- After you speak, some audience members may come up to say hello or ask questions. If they smell alcohol on your breath, they will not assume that you just had one or two drinks to calm your nerves. Instead, they will assume you are Otis, the Mayberry town drunk from "The Andy Griffith Show."

By now you may be thinking that I want you to die of dry mouth. Not at all. In fact, it is important for you to drink more liquid than usual before speaking and sometimes while you are speaking. The real question is not whether to drink but WHAT to drink.

We have already scratched near-boiling drinks. Ice water is on the other extreme. Unfortunately, too much coldness can tense up your vocal cords. Think of them like a rubber band. They are less flexible when frozen than when warm. So the very best thing for your voice is room-temperature water. If you are speaking for more than 10 minutes or you are a guest on a talk-radio or TV show for more than one 10-minute segment, have a glass of room-temperature water by your side at all times.

Your vocal cords will thank you.

Protect Your Voice

Your voice is your most precious speaking instrument. You must preserve and protect it at every opportunity.

Here are several steps to follow to conserve the strength and quality of your voice before a major speech or presentation:

1. Don't sing in the car while listening to the radio. This strains your voice.
2. Don't talk on the telephone.
3. Don't talk at all, except when necessary.
4. Don't smoke.
5. Don't allow yourself to be around second-hand smoke (stay out of smoky bars in your hotel).
6. Don't ever scream!
7. If you are swimming, be careful not to exhale through your mouth (this will strain your vocal chords). Instead, exhale through your nose.

The voice box can be a fragile instrument. If you are nice to it, your voice will serve you well. If you abuse your voice, it will abandon you when you need it most.

I Hate My Voice!

At least once a week one of my trainees tells me, "I hate my voice." This is usually followed by a solemn declaration that somehow all recording devices distort his or her voice in an unflattering matter.

What's going on here?

Perhaps you have noticed when you hear your own voice on a voicemail or on a home video recording that it doesn't sound like you at all. Actually, it does sound like you, just not the "you" that you are used to hearing.

All of us hear our own voice in a distorted manner, only it's not because we have big or small egos. We hear a distorted voice because the bones in our head manipulate the sound we hear internally. Not only do we hear our voices from the outside, but we also hear an internal sound. The structure of our skulls messes with this sound and muffles it in a way that it doesn't for someone simply hearing us through their ears from across the room (that's not exactly using scientific lingo, but that is the science behind the theory).

Often during my trainings when I play back a video recording of one of my clients, he or she reacts with "that's not how I really sound." Yet, he or she also notices that when their colleagues are

videotaped, the sound they hear when the recording is played back is exactly the same as when the colleague was giving the speech live. The student realizes that there is nothing wrong with the recording device.

When people tell me they hate their voice, they aren't lying. But the real problem for most people is that they are just unfamiliar with their "true" voice, and when they hear their voices for the first time the way other people do, the difference in perception is so great that it's shocking.

It is this disconnect that they don't like, not the actual quality of their voices that they hate.

Very few people have voices so mellifluous that they can make a million dollars a year doing voiceovers for TV commercials. The good news is that you don't have to have a voice like that to be an excellent communicator.

Barbara Walters has a speech impediment, but she makes more than $18 million a year, in part, with her voice. Rudy Giuliani has a lisp, yet he is paid more than $100,000 for an hour of work to give a speech. John McCain has a sibilant "s" problem, yet he is a political and media darling.

If you think your voice is holding you back, chances are you are just obsessing over a nonexistent or minor problem.

GET OVER IT!

Know Your Microphone

When you are giving a presentation, it is important to remember that not every microphone is appropriate for every occasion. Whenever possible, try to avoid microphones that are fixed to a lectern or on a stand and connected to a cord.

Mobility is important to a speaker. The more you move, the more confident and comfortable you will appear to your audience, as long as you are not pacing or rocking back and forth awkwardly.

Therefore, you want to use a wireless microphone anytime you are speaking to more than 30 people in a room. You are faced with two main choices: a handheld microphone or a lavaliere clip-on microphone. Both have advantages and disadvantages.

The handheld microphone gives you greater control over your voice. You can bring the microphone right to your mouth and whisper for affect. Or, you can pull it far away from your mouth and yell

without hurting people's ears. Handheld mics are great for maximum emotional affect. That's why singers and comedians always use handheld microphones. Another advantage with a handheld mic is that it allows you to interact nicely with audience members. By sticking the mic in front of them, you allow their comments to be heard too.

The downside to a handheld microphone is that it takes one of your hands out of commission. This decreases your ability to communicate with your hands and part of your body. This is a major disadvantage for many speakers. Plus, there is something about holding a microphone that can make some people look like second rate stand-up comics.

The advantage of the wireless clip-on microphone is that it allows you to have both of your hands free to gesture. The importance of this can not be overestimated for most speakers. The ability to move both hands freely is quite liberating and goes a long way in making your audience feel as though you are speaking in a friendly, conversational manner.

The disadvantage of a clip-on mic is that your mouth is always about the same distance away from the microphone. Therefore, you cannot whisper or shout for dramatic affect.

Keep in mind that you could use BOTH microphones. Start with a clip-on, hands-free microphone for your prepared remarks, but then use a handheld mic for the question and answer session of your speech. These work nicely together for maximum control and impact.

Chapter 3:
Building A Foundation

Chapter 3:
Building A Foundation

There are some basics you need to think about before you give any presentation. Whether it is five minutes long in front of five people or an hour long in front of two thousands conference attendees, the acronyms WEB DASH will serve as a speech creation system, and is a useful starting point for every presentation.

WEB DASH

> **W**ater Cooler Message
> **E**ngage them with Emotion
> **B**enefits to your audience
>
> **D**ata Dump Avoidance
> **A**ctions
> **S**tories
> **H**andful of Key Points

The **W**ater Cooler Message

What is the starting point for preparing a speech?

For some people, it involves creating a thorough and well thought-out two-page outline. For others, it is a matter of creating 50 large piles of data into 50 complex PowerPoint slides. Moreover, there are those individuals who like to just start writing about everything they've done during the last six months, figuring they will cover all of their bases.

None of these approaches is effective.

If we want to accomplish our goals of getting people to remember our message so that they can act on it and tell others, then it should be our focus from the very beginning. The first step in preparing your speech is to take a step back and try to look at it from the perspective of an audience member. Imagine Ned Flanders, an intelligent and attentive audience member, listening to a 20 to 30 minute speech today. Now, imagine Ned walks into the office tomorrow morning at 8:30 and goes to get a cup of coffee.

In walks Ned's colleague, Marge Simpson, who says, "Ned, I had to take Maggie to school yesterday because she missed her bus, and I got to work two hours late. I missed TJ's presentation. I really wanted to hear what he had to say. What did he say?"

Marge and Ned are now standing next to the water cooler and for the next 30 seconds Ned says, "Well Marge, TJ said...."

What is Ned going to say in 30 seconds about your next presentation?

There are several things Ned is NOT going to do, such as the following:

1. Pull out a lengthy set of notes and start reading them.
2. Enumerate a detailed outline of the speech
3. Highlight all of the numbers given in the presentation
4. Describe in highly abstract terms a dozen key concepts

If we are lucky (and if we prepared), Ned is going to talk for about 30 seconds in normal, everyday language describing a couple of key message points he remembers from yesterday's speech.

That's it.

This is how the human brain processes oral information. If you don't believe me, get out three sheets of paper and write down everything you remember hearing from the last three presentations you heard.

There is a lot of white space left on your paper, isn't there?

The first thing I ask my clients to do before they stand up to give their first videotaped practice speech, "What is your water cooler message?"

Inevitably, their eyes shoot upward as they strain to remember the exact order of a dozen key abstract concepts they want to cover in their speech. I politely tell them that this is not a water cooler message. A water cooler message is what a real person would say to another real person in the real world, so forget the fantasy of someone memorizing your whole speech.

Some of my clients can do a great job of summing up their key message points in under a minute. Others have to fish around for an hour before we can all agree that they have an actual water cooler message. It is an hour well spent.

Your water cooler message is the ultimate final product of your presentation communication process. If you can't figure it out and you are the creator of your speech, the chances are slim that your audience will be able to figure it out. Or worse, each person who heard you has a different water cooler message the next day—your message is now being twisted beyond recognition.

"Hey Ned, what did TJ say in his presentation yesterday?"

"I don't know, but he was so boring I had a nice little cat nap. I felt well-rested the entire day!"

Don't let that happen to you. Before you do any more research or create the first graphic, say out loud, and don't just write down your water cooler message. Furthermore, don't do anything else until you are happy with how it sounds.

Engage With The Heart And Head

Most business speakers talk about what they do all day long with the same passion that other people normally reserve for reading the phone book.

Big Mistake!

If you want to communicate a message to an audience you must operate at two separate levels simultaneously—the head and the heart. Of course, you must have the facts and data on your side. Substance is crucial. You must utilize the brain. If you present one fact after another without any emotion, you will never engage your audience. They need to connect with your heart as well.

Why do you care about the subject you are speaking on? If you don't care (really care), why should anyone in your audience care? For that matter, why shouldn't they fall asleep?

When you are talking about your business, your product, or your job, you are speaking on a subject that you have devoted days, weeks, months, years, and sometimes decades to mastering. Presumably, you have some passion for this subject; otherwise, you would be a garbage man instead.

When preparing your presentations, it is imperative that you ask yourself not only what the key points are that you want to get across to your audience, but also ask how you can convey the emotions and excitement you feel about these subjects.

You don't have to provide a tear-jerking end to your stories, but you do need to let your audiences know when you are surprised, disappointed, shocked, happy, or pleased, and why you feel this way.

Facts do not speak for themselves, regardless of what you might have heard on Dragnet. Facts stick in your audience's memories only when you have surrounded them with their emotional significance.

Until you package your ideas, sincerely, honestly, and with genuine emotions, you will never thoroughly engage your audience.

Benefits, Benefits, Benefits

Most speakers have heard that that they should spell out what benefits they can deliver to their audience members, yet most speakers never do this. Why?

Because most speakers are selfish. They are thinking about what is their message, what their department has accomplished in the last quarter, and what goals they possess. Average and mediocre speakers are thinking from the perspective of me, me, me!

The successful speaker is able to have an out-of-body experience while presenting—this speaker floats from the front of the room all the way to the back of the room and into the body of an audience member. The perspective is entirely different back there.

Bad speakers think the facts speak for themselves and that the audience is "smart;" therefore, they can deduce what the benefits are if the speaker simply lays out the facts.

This is total nonsense.

Audiences can only successfully accomplish one task. They can either listen to your presentation, or they can analyze it. They can't do both of these things at once. Don't make your audience work hard—spell out for them in explicit detail what benefits you bring to them.

The skilled speaker realizes that an audience never perceives him to be condescending or "talking down" to them simply for explaining how they can benefit from the message of the presentation. On the contrary, audiences appreciate it when you show concern for their needs and desires.

Many speakers start to explain benefits, but only in a highly abstract manner. They talk about "optimized revenue potential" instead of saying, "Sally, that means you could make an additional $35,000 this year." The first is an abstract fact, the second is a benefit.

The trick for any skilled speaker is how to personalize data in such a way that audience members can relate to it and remember it. By pointing out what benefits your audience members will receive if they buy in to your premise, you will make your message have its ultimate impact.

So, when preparing your speech, be sure to pretend you are an audience member for one moment and ask yourself, "How can this message personally benefit me?" Then, develop a darn good answer.

<u>D</u>ata Dump Avoidance

What do most people do when they find out they have to give a major presentation in two months? For all practical purposes, they get a giant wheelbarrow and start roaming the halls of their office, filling it up with every research report, magazine article, spread sheet, graphics, and old PowerPoint slides they can find. Finally, when the wheelbarrow is stacked so high it is about to tip over, this person types up every fact accumulated, then converts them into bullet points on PowerPoint slides. Abracadabra, and you now have a three-hour speech that, if you speak very, very quickly, you can deliver in 30 minutes.

Whew! That was easy, right?

Unfortunately, what happened here was not a speech or a presentation; instead, it was a data dump. Audiences hate them. You hate them. And yet, many of us continue to give them. The thinking goes something like this:

"I'm nervous about this speech. I don't want to be criticized for leaving anything out. I want to cover my a**, so I'll just include every single thing my department has done for the last quarter. That way I will have covered all my bases, and no one can attack me."

This is a purely defensive position that is destined to bore your audiences and ensure that you communicate nothing to them.

It is fine to accumulate lots of data when you are researching your speech. But, as the speaker, it is your job to be the editor and the sifter of information. It is your job to figure out what is most important, because your audience doesn't have the time or the interest in learning as much about the subject as you do. If they did, they would be giving the speech instead of you.

It is clinically proven that audiences forget 93 percent of what they hear. If you simply present hundreds of data points, each no more than once, your audience will remember very little, and no two people will remember the same points.

What's the solution?

Narrow your message points down to the five most important. Then, give numerous examples, and tell stories fleshing out each point.

Bring your data to life! Don't just dump it on the conference room floor, where it will be stepped on and quickly forgotten by your audience.

Get Some ACTION

Unless you are a college professor or a comedian, the goal of every presentation you make should be to get your audience members to take some sort of ACTION. It could be to sign a contract, buy your product, work longer hours, focus on quality, wear hard hats, invest in your company, or something similar.

Don't be shy about asking people to do what you want.

The problem most speakers have is that they just lay out all of the facts, perhaps the features of their product or service, and they hope people connect all of the dots, and then they ask them to buy the product or contract for services. This is a mistake. When your audience is listening to you, they typically aren't analyzing and synthesizing as well. Your audience can do one thing at a time. Don't force your audience to come to the conclusions you want or to guess at what actions you want them to take.

Spell it out.

When it comes to asking your audience to take action, the more specific and less abstract you are, the better. Regardless of your opinions of televangelists, the successful ones are good at what they do, in part, because of the high degree of specificity in their requests.

Jerry Falwell does not simply ask his TV viewers to send him money. That is a request for action, but it is too vague to garner results. Instead, he says something like this:

"I want you to get up out of your chair right now and go over to your desk. Pull out your checkbook. Find a pen, and write out the check for $100. Make it payable to 'The Old Time Gospel Hour.'

Next, I want you to find an envelope. Put that check in the envelope, and put a stamp on it. Now, before you put it down and go into the kitchen and fix yourself a ham sandwich, I want you to write down the address you see on your screen now on the front of the envelope. Then, I want you to walk out your front door and put the stamped envelope in your mailbox so that your mailman can pick it up tomorrow morning."

That is a highly specific call to action that gets results.

When I give this example to my speech training clients, some of them invariably respond, "But TJ, you are wanting me to sound like some cheesy TV preacher preying upon little old ladies to steal their Social Security checks. I could never be so unscrupulous."

And I respond, "You are missing the point. Don't confuse the subject matter with the process. If you believe that your product or

service is ethical, honest, and legitimate, then you should believe that getting people to buy into what you are selling can only help them. Therefore, the easier you make the process for your audience, the more everyone wins."

Take a good look at the text of your next speech. If you don't have specific calls to action, get out your rewrite pen and get to work.

Tell Your <u>S</u>tory

Of all the tips I give my clients, the most important is to tell stories that flesh out your key message points. The concept of "telling stories" confuses many people. I often have clients tell me, "I'm not a natural story teller."

Or, "I agree with the idea of telling stories in principle, but it just doesn't seem appropriate in our business situations. And besides, there is not enough time."

Sadly, this shows a misunderstanding of what story telling is all about. Let's clarify what stories are not:

- Stories don't have to be funny
- They don't have to be long (30 seconds is often enough)

- They don't have to be about famous people or based in well-known places
- They don't have to be worthy of winning a Pulitzer Prize

It is important that your stories have a message, a resolution, a setting, one person, dialogue, another person, a problem, emotion, and passion. These form the acronym MR. SODA PEP-see more about this in a later section.

Stories are not the most efficient way of communicating data, which is why most business communicators strip out all stories from their speeches. However, stories are the most efficient way of getting audience members to remember what you said.

If your goal is to get people to remember your key points, stories are essential. If you don't care if people remember anything you say, then just present facts and bullet points in a straightforward manner.

If you don't care if people remember your points, why bother giving a presentation in the first place?

Don't Be Greedy,
One Handful Per Customer

If there is one image that I try to get my presentation-training clients to focus on before they start to give a speech, it is the hand. You have five fingers and five key points. If you shoot for more than five, you are just being greedy, like that time in second grade when you tried to take four handfuls of candy on Halloween from that neighbor who just left the bowl of Snicker's bars on the front porch.

Remember, five fingers and five points (or fewer), even if you are speaking for an hour. This idea is confusing to many people. I'm not saying you can only mention five facts, or that you have to say the exact same thing over and over again in a thirty-second loop. You need to have no more than five MAIN points in your presentation. The other points, facts, asides, and tidbits are there to make your five main points more memorable. You should present all other data with the understanding that most people will forget it, and you should be OK with that.

Invariably, one of my clients will protest, "But TJ, I have so much important information that I simply must present. There is no rational or logical way for me to narrow it down to five main points."

I then ask the client, "Can you tell me about the best and most memorable speaker you've heard in the last year?"

After a moment or two of reflection, a name is usually put forward. "Now," I say, "Please tell me every single message point you remember from this person's speech."

What follows is usually a thirty-second summary of, at most, a couple of points. Then, I point out, "Here's the best speech you've heard in a year. You've already admitted that most speeches you hear are not memorable at all. And here's this one speech you think was so great and you can only remember a couple of points, right?"

Trainee: "Uh huh."

"So, if we know that, even if (and this is in an ideal situation) we have impressed our audience into thinking we are in the top 1 percent of speakers, they are only going to remember a couple of points, then why not focus all of our energy on trying to those are more memorable for them?"

Now we are ready to go back to the speech script or outline to start scratching off whole sections and begin the hard work of making just a handful of key points truly memorable.

End With A Bang!

Many a good speech was ruined when the speaker just ran out of gas at the end and mumbled,

"Thank you."

Or

"That's it."

Or

"That's all of my presentation."

What a letdown. The strongest impression you have on your audience is the first impression, the couple of minutes in your speech opening. The second strongest impression you have on any audience is the final impression, the last thing you say and do in front of them.

"But TJ, isn't it rude not to thank my audience?"

Certainly you can thank your audience, just don't make those your final words. Thank people in the middle of the speech somewhere

within the context of an important point. Don't just tack it on at the end because you can't think of anything else to say.

Part of the problem with ending a speech with a mere "thank you" is that it's what your audience is expecting because that is when most boring speakers show their appreciation. "Thank you" has become a cliché at the end of a speech.

If the last thing people hear out of your mouth is a cliché, then the only thing they will remember about you is that you speak clichés. How does that help you promote your message or your reputation?

There is no one perfect formula for the ideal closing of a speech. It doesn't have to involve a poignant story, a clever riddle, or a tie back to an opening theme, even though all of the aforementioned can be great devices.

The first requirement of a great closing is that it be INTERESTING. The second requirement is that you leave your audience thinking about something they have learned. The final requirement is that you ask people to do something and that they feel motivated to actually do it.

Once you do all of those things, then stop, smile, and don't say a word. Not one "Thank you." Not one "You've been a great audience." Just keep silent, smile, and look confident. Then, your

audience will know you are finished, and they will likely start clapping.

The only "thank you's" heard in the room now will be from audience members saying it to you after your speech.

Shorter Isn't Always Sweeter

I have clients come to me each week for training who say that one of their goals is to become more concise when they present. They feel they ramble or talk too long. They want me to teach them how to speak faster and get their points across more quickly. Some even do their homework and point out how Abe Lincoln's Gettysburg Address was only two minutes long, while the politician who spoke before him rambled on and on for two hours.

Do I help these clients with their goals?

No.

Here's why: most of the time the real problem is not that people aren't concise or quick enough. The problem is that people are nervous presenting, and they think that if they can just talk faster, they can sit down sooner and end their discomfort of public speaking. They also feel that if they just speak quickly and end

suddenly, no one will notice that they were nervous, scared, or ill-prepared.

Sadly, this is not the case.

My experience is that most people who feel they speak too long and that they need to shorten their speech never actually speak too long in the first place. The fact that they are nervous changes their perspective of time. They are only talking for three minutes but because they are so uncomfortable, it seems like it has been 10 minutes.

I'm not denigrating the ability to be concise. However, being concise should never be your primary goal when you have the task of communicating. Your main goal is to actually communicate. Striving to be concise, quick, or short can hinder your ability to do this.

Focusing on being concise can be helpful, though, if you discipline yourself to narrow your 50 key points down to five or even three points. Once you have narrowed your key points down to a small and manageable number, your focus should now be exclusively on how to make your key points more memorable, interesting, relevant, and beneficial to your audience. This is where you need to bring in examples, anecdotes, and stories—the very things people tend to drop in their quest to be quick and concise.

Therefore, don't strive to be quick. Instead, be quick to leave a lasting impression—even if it takes a while.

Give Your Presentation
Don't Talk About Your Presentation

Nothing screams out "amateur hour" more than a presenter who insists on talking about his "presentation" in front of his audience. It begins with a speaker who starts off by saying, "Today I would like to talk about..."

This is completely useless and boring information, for three reasons:

1. Your audience knows it is "today."
2. The audience knows it is you. You don't have to tell them.
3. Your audience can figure out that you are talking (we see your lips moving).

The "presentation" is a concept that is relevant only to the speaker, not the audience. Your audience isn't thinking about your "presentation." Instead, they are "in the moment," and they are thinking either, "This person is saying something interesting and useful to me, so I'd better listen carefully," or "This person is a

bore, so I can tune out and think about what I'm going to have for dinner instead."

When a speaker gets up and starts saying things like, "I hope my slides are in the right order this time," or "When I gave this presentation in Chicago last week, the audio didn't work properly," it has a devastating effect on audiences. The audience correctly deduces that you are not focused on them; rather, you are focused on yourself.

Every time you reference your presentation or how you prepared your presentation or difficulties you are having in your presentation, you are wasting valuable time you could be using to tell your audience something interesting and useful to them.

Don't talk about what you are going to say later or at the end of your presentation or how you dreaded thinking about planning the presentation. Just talk about the actual substance that is of interest to your audience.

Focus on your audience, not your "presentation."

Flow Schmo

Many of my corporate executive training clients come to me and express concerns about how their presentation will "flow." They are obsessed with each and every thought connecting in a seamless manner, as if they were writing a work of great literature.

All things being equal, of course it would be nice if every single thought out of your mouth flowed together during a speech. But, not all things are equal. There is a much bigger danger for the average corporate speaker than "flow." The danger is that the speaker is BORING AS HADES!

Your first concern as a speaker is figuring out how you can present information in an interesting and memorable manner. This should be a much bigger concern than whether all of your ideas "flow" together perfectly.

If you have just told an interesting story that makes a point during your speech, there is nothing wrong with simply stopping, pausing, looking at another part of the room, and then starting an entirely new point. Your audience cannot judge your "flow" or your connections in the same way they could if they were reading a written report. When it comes to text, flow is critically important. When sentences and paragraphs don't flow together well, it makes the writer stand out as amateurish, or worse, a poor thinker.

Transitions are not AS important when giving public speeches (note: I am NOT saying that transitions are completely unimportant). This is because people listen differently than they read. When you read, you can stop, go back to the previous paragraph, reflect, and analyze as you go, taking your time doing it. When you listen to someone speak, you are in the moment. You are paying attention to the words as they come out. You don't have the luxury of playing back what was just said or fast-forwarding to a later part of the speech. If you stop to critique some part of the speech, you miss what is being said in the present, and you can never get that moment back.

Being an audience member is a totally different experience from being a reader. The master speaker realizes this. Therefore, the speakers who excel spend most of their time making sure their messages and their stories are truly interesting and memorable. Concern for "flow" is not abandoned, but it is given a back seat.

In The Moment

To truly excel as a communicator in front of an audience, you must project that you are "in the moment." That means you have to be so comfortable with what you are speaking about -and how you are speaking- that nothing can bother you, and you can react and change course in less than a second.

Nervous speakers are so focused on a prepared speech that they wouldn't notice if half of their audience fell over from heart attacks. An in-the-moment speaker is constantly analyzing the eyes and body language of individual audience members. If you are truly in-the-moment, you can alter, adjust, fine tune, stop, speed up, or slow down instantly because you are reading your audience. That means you are so comfortable you can toss out an idea that comes to your head instantly, or react to an audience member's reaction on the spot. An in-the-moment speaker is never thrown for a loop by a question from an audience member because he or she is focused 100 percent on the question of the moment, and is not preoccupied by what they will be saying in five to 10 seconds.

All great communicators create a conversational feel when speaking to their audiences, and nothing simulates the feel and look of an actual conversation more than appearing to be in-the-moment with the person listening to you, whether it is your spouse over the

breakfast table or 10,000 people listening to you in a convention hall.

It takes more than a few moments to become in-the-moment. Don't expect to attain this level on your first, or even tenth, major speech or media appearance. It takes time and persistence. But it is well worth the effort, for you and your audiences.

Avoid The Weasel Words

Many business communicators lard up their speeches with jargon and weasel words. The result? They sound like bureaucratic stooges.

Your goal when speaking is to communicate a message in the clearest and simplest manner possible, while building your reputation as an effective communicator.

For many business people, bad rhetorical habits are acquired somewhere in the second year of business school or after having attended a third annual board of directors meeting.

Here are some of the worst offending clutter phrases:

"*Going forward...*" What an utterly useless phrase! Use "in the future" instead. You wouldn't tell your teenage son, "Going

forward, please keep your room straight," so why use it in a speech or presentation? The sole purpose for using a phrase like "going forward" in a speech is to create the impression that you are saying something fancier than you are actually. So please, going forward, never use the phrase "going forward."

"If you will." This phrase is tacked onto the back of a sentence as if to say, "look at this most original and brilliant insight I have just come up with, as it will require you to change your whole conception of the universe, if you will be so kind as to indulge me in this experiment." Pretentious drivel! Imagine a trap door, if you will, that will spring open and devour you if you ever use the phrase "if you will" in a public speech.

"As it were." See above.

There is nothing wrong with using specialized language to convey complex topics to sophisticated audiences, but that is not what many business communicators do. Instead, they use complex phrases to communicate simple concepts because they are under the delusion that this makes them sound more professional. The simpler and more conversationally you can speak, regardless of how complex the topic is, the greater your audiences will understand, respect, and appreciate you and your message.

Consistency Isn't So Foolish

The biggest problem most of my clients have who seek speech training is that they change the way they talk once the video camera is on them or when they stand up to practice a speech. Most people come in and sit down and are relaxed. They communicate expressively with hand motion, body motion, eyebrow movement, facial movement, and their voices are conversational. So far, so good.

But the second I say, "Let's now do a practice interview or speech, and we will record it," a transformation occurs. It's like when Dr. David Banner turns into the incredible Hulk, only in reverse. Business executives who were engaging, confident, loud, and alive, shrink before my eyes. Their speaking volume decreases. Their voices flatten. Their hands stop moving. The body becomes stiff. The head is frozen. Getting very sleepy…..

What's happening here?

Nerves make people change their normal presentation styles. When you are nervous, you tend to stiffen up. The results are disastrous when it comes to trying to give a good impression to anyone watching you.

The other reason people change how they talk during speeches or media interviews is the mistaken belief that a so-called "formal" presentation requires a more "formal" style of speaking, as was discussed earlier.

Great speakers, however, change very little in their speaking style, regardless of venue, medium, or audience size. Bill Clinton speaks the same way, whether it is to one person, 10 thousand in a room, or 10 million on TV. He is conversational, natural, and relaxed in each speaking situation. Ronald Reagan in his prime was exactly the same way.

So much of my challenge with my speaking clients is getting them to stop changing their normal speaking style once they are standing in front of an audience. People erroneously think that a media coach teaches clients to "act" in a more "theatrical" manner; however, this is not so.

This is one reason why it is relatively easy for most people to become dramatically better speakers and media communicators in a short period of time. For the most part, it does not require learning a tremendous amount of difficult new skills. Instead, it is about taking what you already do well in one arena and using it in another. This is why you can be media trained in one full day, but not learn how to play the guitar well in one day.

Of course, there are some subtle changes that need to be made by speakers, depending on the venue. If you are in a large room with 1,000 people in the audience, you need to speak slower than usual, with slightly longer pauses. This is because it physically takes longer for your sound to travel around the room. Plus, your gestures need to be slightly bigger than usual to be seen. But, other than those minor changes, you need to stick with a conversational tone in your voice and continue to move naturally.

When it comes to communicating well to audiences and the media, there is nothing foolish about consistency, as long as you are consistently conversational and fluid. This is true if you want to be President or just a more persuasive hobgoblin.

Chapter 4:
Once Upon A Time. . .

Chapter 4:
Once Upon A Time...

Most business executives are highly confused as to what is, exactly, a story. They know it must be good, but they assume that they don't have the skills or time to tell one. Nothing could be further from the truth. A story need be neither funny nor long—it can even be delivered in less than 20 seconds. MR SODA PEP. This acronym outlines the elements good stories possess and will guide you in the creation of your own story.

MR SOD PEP

*M*essage
*R*esolution

*S*etting
*O*ne Person
*D*ialogue
*A*nother Person

*P*roblem
*E*motion
*P*assion

What Is The <u>M</u>essage?

When you are telling a story, anecdote, or joke to an audience, it is imperative that you have a message point that is being brought to life. Unless you are rich and famous, nobody cares about the details of your life unless it reveals lessons that are applicable to all.

If you tell a joke, and it makes an important point, then it doesn't have to be hysterically funny. But, if you tell a joke without a point, you are just another amateur at open mic night—and that can be painful.

Make sure your story has a message. It's OK to spell out exactly what the message is before or after you tell a story or both. Ideally, your story is so powerful and memorable that you won't even have to tell your audience what is "the moral of the story" because it will be abundantly obvious.

You should never have to come up with message points as an excuse to tell interesting stories. Instead, your message points are what count and should be the basis for the story. Your stories serve as learning and memory devices for your audience so that your messages do not float away into the ether after your speech has concluded.

Your mother may think you are witty, and your friends may think of you as a brilliant conversationalist, but an audience that does not know you will not be as easily impressed. You must minimize your risk by simultaneously communicating at several levels: intellectually with message points, emotionally with stories about real people, and visually by describing stories. One of these methods is bound to work.

Remember, the professional storyteller tells stories with the goal of entertaining. The successful communicator tells stories with the goal of communicating a message. (Hint: It's a lot easier to be a successful communicator than it is to be a professional storyteller.)

Have A Resolution, Happy Or Otherwise

When telling stories to your audience, it is critical to have a resolution. How does your anecdote end? How were the critical issues resolved? Too many speakers have a perfectly good beginning to a story, but then they get lost. They become sidetracked. They forget to finish. They ramble.

It is not important that your stories have a happy ending. You are not trying to market-test a blockbuster movie with a pre-fab "they lived happily-ever-after" ending.

The important thing is that your audience is able to see how the described conflict with your top client or difficult employee has now been resolved and a lesson was learned in the end.

Too many speakers like to describe conflict or whine about problem situations. These can be important parts of telling a story, but they don't serve the grander purpose of communicating your message. Rather, you must describe a clear-cut ending where the resolution illustrates an important concept.

Don't leave your audience hanging, and don't introduce clients, customers, colleagues, and prospects in your speech unless you are willing to detail what happens to them within the immediate context of your story. If your audience is left wondering whatever happened to Mr. Smith in accounting because you discussed his problem three minutes ago but never resolved it, then they are less likely to be focused on what you are saying right now. They are still lost trying to figure out what happened earlier.

The less you distract your audience, the better. You want your audience focusing on exactly one thing at a time: what you are saying at that moment. That is why you don't want to leave any holes or gaps in your logic or your narrative, hence the need for an ending to each story.

It doesn't have to be a STRONG ending in a Hollywood sense or even be happy or poignant. It just has to end in a way that makes some sort of sense and helps prove one of your message points.

It Was A Dark And Stormy Night. . .
Setting

It was a dark and stormy night, and I was alone in a large haunted mansion.... When you are telling a story in the middle of a presentation, it is imperative that you take the time to describe your physical setting. It doesn't have to be an exotic locale. It could be as simple as, "I was sitting in my office one day about to leave for lunch when the phone rings. I pick it up, and it's Smithers in Investor Relations..."

Of course this isn't the beginning of an epic novel, but it could work in a presentation because most members in your audience can relate to the setting and visualize it because they all have offices and phones, and all have received phone calls before going to lunch. Therefore, your audience doesn't just hear your words; instead, they "see" your words.

The human memory is profoundly affected by the visual, much more so than by auditory.

Do you doubt me? Then ask yourself this: What is easier to remember, someone's face or a name? You see a face, whereas you only hear a name. Make your audience "see" your speech through descriptive details of the physical settings of your stories.

When you are telling a story to make a point during a presentation, describing the setting plays several crucial roles:

1. Describing a physical setting makes it less abstract and therefore more memorable.

2. It will create images in the minds of your audience members. Instead of you doing all of the work during the presentation, your audience is doing half the work by providing the visual imagery in their own minds. (A good speaker is smart and lazy the way Tom Sawyer was when painting a fence.)

3. When describing a setting, you have no choice but to slow down the introduction of new concepts, thus making it easier for your audience to focus on the main concept of your story. Describing settings slows down the entire pace of a speech, which is a good thing because most business presenters race to see how much data they can cover in a short period of time.

4. It is very easy on the speaker's memory. It is the same for the audience. When you as the speaker can "see" what it is you are talking about, you are less likely to have to look at

notes, papers, slides, or upward in a vain attempt to remember your outline on the TelePrompTer in your brain.

5. It gives your audience the chance to be less than perfect, as there are no perfect audiences unless you are a minister on Sunday morning and the offerings overflow the collection plate. If the audience zones out for a second or doesn't understand something you've said, it won't matter because they merely lost a part of the setting.

Mediocre speakers routinely fail to describe the settings of their stories. They reason, "I don't have time for that. I have too many important points to get across in a short period of time." In reality, however, you have a short period of time to make a MEMORABLE impression on your audience. Setting the stage for a story is a crucial element in making your message resonate in your audiences' memories.

Introduce One Person
The Star Of Your Show

When you are telling a story to make a point during a presentation, you need to introduce characters. Start with one person, ideally you. When you personalize your story, you make it more interesting to your audience, and they will be able to relate to you better.

It's not about you having a big ego or trying to be boastful, but by introducing yourself as a character in your story, you make it more authentic. When you fail to personalize your presentation with stories that directly involve you, your speech takes on a canned generic quality, as if a nameless, faceless bureaucrat in the speech writing department wrote it for a nameless, faceless executive to be delivered to any audience.

Ho, hum.

Don't just tell people the facts. Tell them how you felt when you were in a conversation with a client, customer, or colleague when you found out the facts and their relevance. By introducing yourself as a character in your story, you help slow down the onslaught of new facts in a presentation, and you make it easier for each audience member to process the new information you are delivering. By showing how you reacted to new concepts, you make it much simpler for every single person to identify with them as well.

You may be looking at the last couple of paragraphs I wrote and are scratching your head thinking, "What kind of touchy-feely mumbo jumbo is TJ blathering about? Is he talking about a speech to simpletons?"

No, I am talking about a speech you might give to an audience in which everyone has a PhD from M.I.T. It is the nature of audiences to have a much harder time understanding what you say versus what they read or study. Simplifying your information by presenting it through the eyes of one person will greatly improve your audience's understanding of your message.

"And She Said To Me, '...' "
<u>D</u>ialogue

The most important element of telling a story to flesh out your point to an audience is the use of dialogue.

But, what is dialogue?

Don't say: "My colleague Jane expressed to me her displeasure with my music selection and asked that I turn it down."

This is not dialogue!

Instead, say: "Jane marched into my office and said, 'Hey TJ, that's the worst music I ever heard in my life. Please turn it off, or I'm going to throw your stereo out the window.' And I said, 'Calm down Jane. I'll turn it down.'"

This is dialogue.

Most of us use dialogue quite naturally when we are telling our friends and families interesting stores about what happened throughout our day. Many great, humorous stories are told in a dialogue format. Yet, the first thing most business presenters do is strip the dialogue out of presentations because they think it is not "professional" or "businesslike." Nothing could be further from the truth. Of course, it is possible to say things that are unprofessional during a presentation, but that has to do with the content of what you are saying, not because you said it in an interesting manner.

When you tell a story using dialogue, several positive things occur at once:

1. By introducing another character, you make your story more interesting.
2. Speaking in dialogue takes you away from the position of a God-like narrator from above and puts you down on the ground in a non-abstract position for your audience.

3. When you say the words that someone else said to you, you change the tone of your voice. This makes you less monotonous.

4. When you insert dialog, you naturally pause between characters. This pausing makes you sound more conversational and interesting.

5. By using dialog, you are, by definition, making your presentation more conversational, less abstract, and, therefore, easier to follow.

6. Further, by using dialog, you are slowing down the delivery of new facts to your audience, thus giving them a chance to catch up and absorb your most important points.

Still, it is possible to give a good presentation without using stories with dialog, but you are making it much harder on yourself if you try. All great speakers sprinkle dialogue throughout their presentations, no matter how complex, difficult, or technical the subject matter. All lousy, boring speakers studiously avoid the use of dialogue.

Which camp do you want to join?

What Is Your Problem?

All good Broadway dramas have huge conflicts for their stars to overcome. All interesting stories have some internal conflict or problem for the central figures to address. Your story must also have a clear-cut problem to solve.

When telling your story, an important element is that you be as specific and graphic as possible. Don't describe your problem abstractly or generically.

Don't say, "We had connectivity issues."

Do say, "We had a hole in our gas pipe, and if we didn't fix it within an hour, we were in danger of going up in flames."

What is your problem? More specifically, what is the problem you are solving for other people? If you are in business, what problem do you solve that people are willing to pay you money to remedy? If you are in politics, what problem in society are you trying to fix? A strong story spells out a problem in a clear-cut, compelling, and possibly visual manner. Once you have laid this out, you have created anticipation for your solutions.

If your message is nothing but problems, you are nothing but a complainer. However, if you can articulate a specific problem and

immediately follow it up with a compelling solution, then you are on your way to becoming a master communicator.

It's OK To Wear Your
Emotions On Your Sleeve

It's good to express emotions when you are telling stories to your audience in addition to the obvious showing of passion for your work and your company. By expressing emotion, you make people understand how you feel about events you experience.

You could exhibit surprise, fear, disappointment, excitement, or shock.

The important thing is that you reveal to your audience that you are a human being with feelings, not just a computer spewing out dots and dashes.

Some business leaders reading this section are scoffing, "That's not professional. I'll be a laughing stock if I wear my emotions on my sleeve."

No, you won't.

If you look at many of the premier business leaders of the last quarter of a century, whether it is Jack Welch of General Electric or John Akers of IBM, you will see that they spoke with great emotion in all of their presentations to employees, shareholders, media, and public.

In my experience as a presentation coach, insecure people are afraid to show their emotions. Secure individuals are comfortable showing their emotions while telling stories in their presentations. The secure presenter understands that audiences will connect more with them when the human element is introduced. Besides, reasons the secure executive, if the audience doesn't like it, too bad. It is still a risk worth taking.

Emotion is clearly an essential element of any story you tell, as long as you don't become over-sentimental or sappy.

I'M NOT SAYING YOU HAVE TO CRY IN THE MIDDLE OF YOUR SPEECH TO YOUR BOARD OF DIRECTORS. It's not about tears or biting your lip or revealing devastation.

Showing emotion in a story can be as simple as sharing how happy and surprised you were when you found out that you beat last quarter's earnings estimates by 15 percent!

Like everything else you say and do during a presentation, your use of emotion should be with a purpose. By revealing your emotions when telling stories to your audience, you give people a better sense of what is important to you, thus making your key points more memorable.

So, feel free to laugh, smile, gawk, or frown away!

The Passion Premium

All good stories reveal some moment of passion on the part of the speaker. It doesn't have to involve yelling or screaming or anything phony, but it should convey to people that you have a passion for whatever it is you are talking about.

If you aren't passionate about your subject matter, why should anyone else care about your topic? Too many people give a presentation and convey the same amount of enthusiasm as someone reading a telephone book.

Blah!

Bad communicators communicate exclusively at the intellectual level. Great communicators consistently communicate at both the

intellectual AND emotional levels. Further, the best way to do this is by communicating your message with passionate stories.

Too many business executives feel that they will appear to be unprofessional if they use any passion when speaking. We've all seen the stone-faced executive with the grave voice plow though numbers and facts in a flat, monotone, and lifeless manner. This impresses no one.

Passion is an emotion that is ideal for showcasing your commitment to a particular set of ideals or course of action. If you are trying to convince your audience to take a particular set of actions or buy into your opinions, you need to convince them not only that you believe that what you are telling them is true, but that you are also passionate in this belief. Only then will you have the ultimate credibility as a messenger.

So, You Want To Be A Comedian

Nothing is better than when you can make a live audience breakup with laughter while you are giving a speech. Yet, nothing is worse than attempting humor and failing.

Many beginner and intermediate speakers feel like they have to have some humor in their speech, particularly at the beginning, or their

speech will be a failure. This is not so. You can be a great speaker and never, ever get laughs.

If you are going to attempt humor, there are several guidelines you should follow:

1. Don't tell jokes. "Joke" telling is a tough skill to master. Most standup comics work on it nightly for years before they master the proper technique. If you tell a joke, don't act like you know it is a joke, and make sure you have a personal connection to it.

2. Never telegraph a joke or humorous anecdote. Don't say, "I'd like to tell you a humorous story about...." Simply tell the story. Your audience will decide whether or not it's humorous. If you announce you are trying to tell something funny, you eliminate the element of surprise, which is crucial to humor. Plus, you immediately increase your audience's expectations. When you announce that a story is going to be funny, a certain percentage of your audience is going to think, "Well, I'll be the judge of whether or not it's funny."

3. Don't start your speech with a funny story or joke. Many in your audience will expect you to tell a joke at the beginning, so use of the technique has become cliché. It's OK to plan to use a humorous story, but place it in the middle or near the end.

4. Don't tell well-known humorous stories or anecdotes. Everyone has heard the one about the boat that thought the lighthouse was another boat. Don't tell it again. All humor needs to appear to be a natural part of who you are and what you do. Otherwise, you will seem like a second-rate comic who just got kicked out of the Catskills.

5. Don't use humor that isn't specific to some point you are trying to make. If you are telling a funny story just to be funny, the stakes become much higher. It takes the speech out of context and leads your audience to focus on the comedy instead of the message. When this happens, at a subconscious level, your audience is now comparing you to other professional comics like Jerry Seinfeld. I don't know about you, but I don't want to compete with Jerry Seinfeld. That is not a battle you or I will win.

The best way to use humor in a speech is to simply tell a real life story where something funny happened to you. You know it is funny because when you relayed the incident to friends and family, they laughed hard. Now, when you tell it in front of a large audience, you are likely to get a laugh. Even if they don't laugh, it won't seem like you flopped because you were simply telling a story to make your point. You won't seem like you were trying to be funny in the first place; therefore, how could you flop?

Go break a leg!

Chapter 5:
PowerPoint

Chapter 5:
PowerPoint

PowerPoint Is The Greatest
Invention Ever Created For Speakers

Except for the 99.999 percent of the time when it is used incorrectly.

PowerPoint is increasingly gaining a bad reputation as a speaker tool. However, I believe this is unjust. It's sort of like you saying all television is awful when yours has been upside down in your living room for the past 10 years. The fact that you didn't use your TV effectively doesn't mean that all TV is lousy.

PowerPoint slides can be quite effective when used properly as an enhancement to a speaker's presentation. The key word here is "enhancement." There is actually no such thing as a "PowerPoint Presentation." There are some people who give presentations and use PowerPoint slides to make a better and more memorable impression on an audience, although this is an extremely rare phenomenon. Then, there are the people who use PowerPoint slides to make a bad or unmemorable impression on their audiences (Is this you?).

If you want to become effective at using PowerPoint in your presentations, the first thing you have to do is throw out every thing you think you know about it. This will likely upset the people in your corporate communications department who normally whip up a quick PowerPoint presentation for you that consists of breaking your speech down to 999 bullet points, and then sticking them on slides with your corporate logo and fine print legal disclaimers.

For many people, the current PowerPoint slide system "works" in the sense that they get paid to create or deliver them, no one complains, and everything sort of fits in with what everyone else does. However, the current PowerPoint slide system does not "work" in the sense that any actual ideas were communicated to the audience.

Why didn't communication occur?

The slides were so complex, detailed, abstract, data-filled, and word-packed that it was boring to the audience.

The primary problem of all PowerPoint Presenters is that their audiences fall asleep! If people in the room aren't literally snoring, they have figuratively and mentally checked out. Your monotone reading of a bunch of words next to bullet points on a screen is about as interesting as watching a test pattern on TV. Your audience

is either reading ahead on the screen, reading your handouts, or reading their emails from their PDAs.

Once you dim the lights for a PowerPoint Presentation, if you start reading a bunch of words on a screen, it's only a matter of time before your audience will reach an altered state of consciousness—and it's not euphoria from new insights gleaned from your presentation.

If your audience is sleeping, or even if they are no longer paying close attention, you have failed at every level as a speaker:

A. Your audience is not going to understand you or your message because they aren't paying attention.

B. They aren't going to remember a thing because they didn't hear it in the first place.

C. Your audience isn't going to take the action that you want them to take because they don't even know what action it is that you want them to take.

D. Your audience isn't going to tell other people anything about you or your message other than that you were a bore, and you helped them catch up on nap time.

The main objective when using PowerPoint is to make sure you are not putting your audience to sleep.

PowerPoint is NOT a TelePrompTer

One of the biggest misconceptions about PowerPoint is that it can and should be used as a TelePrompTer. A TelePrompTer is a machine that newscasters use to read their scripts while looking into the camera. The TelePrompTer projects the text in front of the newscaster so that the anchor easily sees it, but it is invisible to the viewers. Politicians also use TelePrompTers. To the audience, the only thing visible is a clear piece of glass. But if you are standing directly in front of the TelePrompTer, where the politician is standing, you can see all of the words of your speech scrolling across the glass.

However, there is one big, huge, gigantic difference between a TelePrompTer and a PowerPoint slide. If you are using a TelePrompTer, your audience doesn't see the text of your speech anywhere. They have to focus on you. If you are comfortable with your words and have practiced often enough, your audience won't even know you are using one. In contrast, with PowerPoint, if you are reading words off of a slide, your audience can also see and read the same words.

The audience no longer needs you. Why? They can read faster silently than you can aloud. You are no longer the star of the show. Instead, you are now a clumsy oaf who is just getting in the way.

A speech is a performance, like it or not. The whole trick to delivering a great performance is to not let your audience see the mechanics of it. If you let them see words on a PowerPoint slide, you are revealing the whole architecture of your presentation. You have taken out all of the mystery.

This is a problem for you because you have now been reduced to the status of boring hack who is insulting the audience by reading to them, as if you were assuming your audience does not know how to read.

Think of how powerful and commanding the Wizard of Oz was to Dorothy and her gang when all they could do was focus on his image and his powerful voice. But, once the wizard was revealed as the little old man behind the curtain pushing around a bunch of buttons and knobs, the image was destroyed. The mystique was removed, and the power was nearly lost.

The second your audience sees you reading words from a PowerPoint slide, you become nothing more than a little man pushing knobs around trying to fool people.

Don't let this happen to you.

When you put words up on a PowerPoint slide, the words are for you. They are tools to make your life easier as a speaker.

Unfortunately, your audience doesn't care about you. They care about themselves. When you put words up on a slide and project them to your audience, you are also projecting the message that you don't care about your audience, and you only care about yourself. This is not a message that is said with the intent to "suck up to" an audience.

You need to use your PowerPoint slides exclusively for images that will enhance your audience's understanding and memory of your key message points. Unfortunately, there is nothing memorable or more understandable about putting a bunch of words on a screen.

So, am I saying that you now have to memorize your entire speech? No, that would be too time-consuming and counterproductive.

Am I suggesting you go out and rent an expensive TelePrompTer machine for thousands of dollars before every presentation you give? No, that isn't practical either.

Instead, Media Training Worldwide has devised a more high-tech, sophisticated, and state-of-the-art solution for your notes and speech outlines.

After years of laboratory research, we came up with an invention we like to call a piece of paper!

That's right, a simple piece of paper. That's all you need. There is nothing wrong with using notes as a speaker. Your notes with your outline and your words are for you only. There is no reason whatsoever to let anyone else see them. As long as you can see them, then they are serving their purpose. Paper is cheap, handy, portable, replaceable, changeable, and you can cut it into any size or shape you want. Therefore, it is unlikely you can come up with anything better than a single sheet of paper.

Feel free to steal my invention. I won't sue you.

Three Presentations In One

Any time you are giving a PowerPoint Presentation, you are really giving three separate presentations, including:

1. The words out of your mouth.
2. The slides you are projecting on the screen.
3. The paper handouts you give to audience members after your presentation is over.

Ideally, each one of your presentations is distinct and 95 percent different from the other presentations. Usually, when I explain this concept to executives who are taking my presentation training

course, people look at me strangely, as if to say, "TJ, what in the he@# are you talking about?"

Each medium is unique, and each one contains inherent strengths and weaknesses. The spoken word is excellent for conveying emotions and stories but is a poor medium for helping people retain large amounts of facts.

Visual projections on a wall or screen are wonderful for conveying images that stick in a viewer's mind and make abstract concepts become more concrete and understandable. Although, projected slides are a poor and inefficient method for getting people to retain large amounts of data.

The printed page is great for conveying large amounts of data. It is the most accessible and flexible of all media because your audience can underline points that pertain to them or find interesting, reread sections, file it away, and then pull it out again three months later to read it again. However, print does not convey the emotion or passion a speaker may have for a subject.

It is also important to point out that a speaker should only give handouts only after they have concluded the speech. Audience members can read faster than a speaker can speak. Thus, any speaker who distributes printed material to an audience before or

during a presentation is guaranteeing that the audience's attention will be distracted and diverted.

One significant myth about PowerPoint is that the slides you project have to be the same as the ones included in your handout. This is absurd. Microsoft PowerPoint has a "notes" function that allows you to include a substantial amount of text and data that does not appear on the projected image but does appear when printed. You should use this function liberally. It is easy for people to read lots of words or columns when they are holding paper in their own hands; conversely, it is hard and awkward to read as much halfway across the room on a big screen. Furthermore, there is nothing wrong with giving attendees handouts that are completely 100 percent different from the projected slides.

The ideal PowerPoint presentation consists of a speaker who gives an interesting and powerful opening two-to-five minute talk before the first slide is ever shown. Then, the speaker makes another interesting point, gives examples, and tells a story. Then, and only then, he shows the next slide that vividly brings the same point home. This sequence follows throughout the speech with the speaker talking in a conversational way, providing examples and telling stories to flesh-out a point followed by a slide that dramatically and visually makes that point. At the conclusion of the speech, the printed handouts are dispersed. Those interested can

read the detailed and text-laden documents on the way home or file them for future reference.

You are probably thinking to yourself now, "This is crazy talk. I've never seen anyone give a PowerPoint that way." You are right. It is an unusual technique. However, it is the most effective way to use PowerPoint if your goal is to actually communicate a message.

Most people don't give three separate presentations when they are using PowerPoint. Instead, the vast majority of people give PowerPoint presentations by more or less saying the same thing that is on their projected slides, and providing handouts that are exactly the same as the projected slides.

Then again, the vast majority of people in the 19th century used leeches to cure their illnesses.

Therefore, don't follow the crowd just to fit in. Instead, focus on making your presentation as interesting and as memorable as possible for your audience by fully exploiting the unique strengths of each medium.

You Aren't Steven Spielberg

One of the worst trends among corporate speakers these days is the use of video during their presentations, especially when it is interspersed among PowerPoint slides.

"But TJ, get with it. This is the MTV Generation. Everything has got to be fast cut, quick edit, with loud thumping rock music behind it. Otherwise, we will lose the audience, right?"

Wrong.

I'm not saying video is always a complete waste of time, but for most speakers, it is nothing more than a crutch.

The following reasons are why video is a bad idea for most speakers:

1. It takes a long time to do a good video. This is time you could be using to prepare AND REHEARSE an actual speech that is interesting.
2. Technically, it is very easy for something to go wrong when presenting a video, leaving you with egg on your face.
3. Even if your video goes well, you won't get the credit, the video will because people will assume some unsung producer in the home office did everything.

4. Video is great for entertaining your audience, but it is unlikely to increase the chances that your message will stick in the audience's memory.

Along with videos possibly being bad for an individual speech, they can also be bad for your long-term reputation. There are two main reasons for this:

1. If people are looking at a video, they aren't looking at you. This means they aren't forming a good image of you as a speaker or as a communicator. Audience members aren't getting a sense of your leadership potential. Instead, they see someone who took the easy way out. You punted.

2. Once you introduce a video element to your presentation, your audience is no longer comparing you to other speakers. Instead, they are subconsciously comparing you to Francis Ford Coppola or Steven Spielberg because you have now entered the realm of video on a big screen. Guess what? That's not a battle you are going to win. By introducing video, you are dramatically raising the standards for yourself because everyone has seen tens of thousands of hours of well-produced video during their lives. What they haven't witnessed are excellent speeches and presentations.

Why go there?

By giving a well-delivered presentation devoid of gimmicks like cutesy video clips, the focus is on you as a speaker and as a communicator. Plus, the audience is no longer comparing you to the Director of *ET*.

Instead, they are now directly comparing you to the last speaker who stood up and bored them, fumbled around, seemed uncomfortable, and then sat down after saying nothing memorable.

That's who I want to be compared to anytime I speak and so should you. Stack the deck in your favor, and you will win the Oscar award for best presentation at your venue.

Don't Betray Your Audience

If your best friend betrays you in your time of need, you say, "He turned his back on me!" Indeed, the very act of turning your back to someone's face is widely seen as an act of betrayal (or at least rudeness).

What is the first thing many presenters do when giving a PowerPoint presentation? They literally turn their backs to their audience. Why does the presenter do this? To read the slides. This is a fiasco for many reasons.

Again, if 93 percent of what is communicated during a presentation comes from facial expressions, posture, hand, head, and eye movement, voice tone, and other body language, then the second you turn your back to your audience, you instantly lose 93 percent of your abilities to communicate with people.

Don't do it!

There is nothing impressive about staring at the back of your head. Do not betray your audience. If the room is configured in such a way that you are between the screen and your audience, this is still no justification for you to turn your back on them while you are talking. The screens are for your audience. They are not for you.

Anytime you are talking, you should be engaged in direct eye contact with an audience member. This way, you can use every element of your verbal and non-verbal communication skills.

If you have your back to your audience, it is boring to people. If you bore them, even if it's not to the point that they fall asleep, your presentation is a bomb.

The only time you should turn your back on your audience, and I mean the ONLY time, is the second you flash up a new screen, and you have stopped talking right after you have introduced the concepts people are about to see displayed on the screen.

If a screen is so complex that you find yourself with a laser pointer wading through it for half an hour, this is usually a good indication that your slide is too complex and needs to be revised.

Make sure your audience can see your entire face and body every second you are speaking. Then, you and your message will make the best lasting impression.

One Thing At A Time

Most PowerPoint Presentations fail because the speaker has set himself or herself up for failure from the very beginning. Speakers intentionally distract their audience members by asking them to do three things at once—listen to the speaker, look at a PowerPoint and read a handout, simultaneously!

This makes as much sense as forcing your third grader to do his math homework while watching television and having the radio on full blast. We all think we are smart enough to multi-task and do10 things at once, but the reality is that we can't. We all like to think that we are multi-talented geniuses, but we aren't. All available research shows that people forget the vast majority of the information they hear and that each additional distraction further diminishes retention.

Your audience members can look at one thing at a time; they can focus on one thing at a time. When you give them three different choices (you, the PowerPoint, the handouts), you are guaranteeing that 2/3 of your efforts are going to fail. Furthermore, you confuse your audience and muddle your message and impact.

The object is to give the audience one single thing to look at and focus on at a time. Your audience can either listen to you or they can read/figure out a PowerPoint slide, or they can read the brochure in their hands. They really can't do all of them at the same time.

The key here is pacing and pausing. When you speak, have no slides up whatsoever. This way your audience has to look at you— there is nothing else interesting to look at in the room. When you want people to look at your slide, then stop talking. That's right, give people a few seconds of total silence or however much time they need to absorb the contents of your slide.

Next is the issue of sequencing. Typically, most presenters throw up a slide and then start talking about the slide while it is still up there. Seemingly, the slides are driving the show, not the presenter. This is not how you want to position yourself as a speaker. Good presenters want the focus to be on their message, not the tools that communicate their message—there is a difference.

The correct way to use PowerPoint is to start with nothing on the screen. First you introduce your concept. Then, you give some facts and examples to back it up. Next, you tell a story that vividly brings your key point to life. Finally, you stop talking and you flash up your slide that communicates the same point, but in a more visual way. After you have given people a chance to look at the slide, you take it down and then you start talking again about a new point, with nothing on the screen to distract your audience. After your presentation is through, then you pass out written information as handouts.

This is not how most PowerPoint Presentations are delivered. In fact, chances are that you have never seen one delivered this way. But this is the most effective way to communicate your message and make a strong impression as a dynamic communicator.

Do one thing at a time, and do it well to become a master communicator.

Whiteout Is Not Just For Typos

As I wrote earlier, the most effective way to use PowerPoint slides is to not have any slides displayed while you are speaking.

How on earth do you accomplish this?

There are three options:

1. After you have finished letting people look at a slide, hit the "w" key on your laptop. The entire projected screen will go white. Your audience must now look at you because there is nothing else at which to look. This whiteout function is a part of the Microsoft PowerPoint software and works on any computer.

2. Press the "b" key on your laptop. The entire projected screen will go black. Again, your audience will have to look at you because it's not very interesting to stare at a black screen. (This also works on any PowerPoint software program.)

In both of the above situations, all you have to do is hit any key and the image you previously had on your screen returns instantly. You then press "enter," "page down," or "shift" to advance to the next screen.

3. The final --and best-- option is to create a blank screen using your same color scheme and background in between every content screen. This way, you can just advance to each screen the way you normally would, and it will immediately rotate between content and blank screens, and all eyes will be back on you. Doing this will prevent you from fumbling around looking for a "b" or "w" key, and it will allow you to present in a highly polished manner.

When you try any of these three techniques, it may feel awkward at first. It may even seem confusing to you, but it won't be confusing to your audience. You will have simplified their lives. Now, your audience doesn't have to make tough choices on where to look or on what to focus. You and your slides will obtain the audience's complete attention when appropriate by maximizing each medium's effectiveness.

You Are The Star Of The Show

Most people believe that a PowerPoint presentation is about the PowerPoint. They figuratively wipe their brow and say, "Whew, what a relief I don't have to give a big speech. I just have to go through some slides."

This is a mistaken notion, one that will do little to advance your career.

A PowerPoint presentation is still about you, the presenter, no matter how modest. During a PowerPoint presentation, you are the star of the show, not the slides, regardless of how well produced are your slides.

If the slides were the most important thing, then you could just email them to everyone in the audience, right?

Like it or not, anytime you give a PowerPoint presentation, all of your audience members are judgmental whether consciously or unconsciously. Nevertheless, they are all judging you on your abilities, knowledge, manner of communication, and short-and long-term career potential.

You can't hide from this reality. In fact, if you try to hide, you will end up getting poor marks in most categories.

PowerPoint Is Your Dessert

Too many presenters act as though they believe their PowerPoint Slides are the main course of their entire presentation. In fact, these presenters act like their slides are every course on the menu.

This is ridiculous!

You as the speaker are the main course of the presentation for your audience. Whether you like it or not, or realize it or not, you are the main course.

So, what is the proper way of thinking of the PowerPoint slides? They are the dessert. Now, I like dessert; in fact, we all like dessert occasionally. Yet, dessert does not make an entire meal. After all, sometimes you eat a great appetizer and a wonderful main course, and you have no room or desire for a dessert.

It is possible to have to have a great meal without having any dessert. However, it is not possible to have a great meal with only a good desert and a lousy main course. A restaurateur who serves the tastiest tarts for dessert but serves only Spam for a main course will soon be out of business.

Once you realize that you are the star of the show (or the main course), you can now focus on one thing: giving your total attention, energy, and intelligence to your audience's comprehension of your message.

The Foreign Language
PowerPoint Solution

Chances are, your PowerPoint slides are lousy and boring. How can you tell for sure?

Show them to someone who doesn't speak your language. If they can't figure out your message, then your slides aren't working. Ideally, PowerPoint slides are visual in nature. They tell a story in images, not words. If you are putting words on a PowerPoint slide, you are wasting time and energy. Words can be more easily heard from you or read from a paper handout, so don't put words on PowerPoint slides!

Successful action movies, like the James Bond 007 series, play well all over the world, and it's not just because of excellent translations or dubs. The movies communicate visually, so it doesn't matter what the subtitles or translations say.

It is the same for great PowerPoint slides.

If you really want to make sure you have an excellent PowerPoint, you should apply two tests to every slide:

1. Can someone who doesn't speak your language understand the meaning and message behind your slide?

2. Is the slide simple enough that if it were a billboard on the highway and you were driving by at 70 miles per hour you be able to understand it?

If the answer isn't yes to both questions, get rid of the slide.

Do Not "Build"

One of the worst offenses you can ever commit when presenting a PowerPoint Presentation is to use a "build." A "build" is when you add an element to the existing slide. In other words, you "build" one more element on top of the existing slide. Typically, this means you add one set of words on top of another set of words.

For example:

(Slide appears with a company logo and text)
"Media Training Worldwide"

(Below the text is just a blank screen)

Now, you hit your "enter" or the "page down" key and instead of an entirely new page coming up, your existing page remains.

Now, something extra pops up:

"• Media and Presentation Training for Executives"

When the "enter" key is hit again, more text emerges below, alongside yet another bullet point.

"• More than 100 media and presentation training DVDs, CDs, and books."

These bullet points can be added indefinitely.

The technology wizards at Microsoft have made this an incredibly easy function to use when you create your PowerPoint slides. At some point, your peers will use builds. In fact, your boss likely uses builds.

Resist the pressure! Don't use builds!

Builds are childish, boring, ineffective, and make you look like a dime-store tipping bird that bobs for water exactly once every three seconds.

Builds are an excellent way to trot out a bunch of boring text onto a slide for someone to read. Why in the world would you want to do this to your audience? They are there to listen to you. If you want them to read one sentence at a time, give them a handout AFTER your presentation is over.

If you want to instantly triple the effectiveness of your presentations and all of the presentations of your colleagues, ban all builds immediately and permanently.

One Idea Per Slide

The PowerPoint slide's greatest enemy is complexity. Presenters include too much information in the normal slide.

People squeeze six graphs onto one slide because it fits. Presenters lard on 57 "builds" on a single slide because they are capable. Speakers use elaborate color codes with keys and footnotes on slides because it's possible.

This doesn't mean they should.

Most people from the time they were three months old started looking at screens from across a room—to watch television. Very few of us grew up reading on screens from across a room. People are accustomed to looking at images, typically one at a time, on a screen. This is the grammar of the screen and the structure of how to communicate in this medium. The producers of Seinfeld didn't try to make it twice as funny by having a split screen segment featuring George and Elaine speaking on one side, while at the very same

time showing a conversation between Jerry and Kramer on the other.

It was one conversation at a time, usually just one person speaking at a time.

Smart business communicators use this same structural technique when using PowerPoint slides. They have each slide communicate no more than one key message point.

The trick to this is to use a visual and NOT a bunch of words. Words are abstractions and are not memorable. Pictures, images, drawings, and cartoons all stick in your audience's memories better.

Thus, select a visual that dramatizes your point and make sure you have no more than one point and one visual per slide. If you have more details or images to share, then put them in the paper handouts that you distribute after your presentation.

Ugly Slides Make
Ugly Presentations

Many people who create PowerPoint slides for their bosses seem to be playing a game called, "Let's see how much useless stuff we can cram on a single slide before anyone notices that we are trying to make them look bad." Yet, no one ever calls him on it.

Too many people write out a conventionally boring speech filled with nothing but boring facts and figures, then they cut and paste this hodgepodge into a PowerPoint slide. Next, to get really fancy and high tech, they stick bullet points in front of every sentence. (That technique will really wow the crowd!)

Or, they will put a bunch of words in little boxes and then connect each box with an arrow to another box, preferably making audience members turn their heads sideways to read some of the fine print. That always works wonders—if you want people to fall asleep (or hurt their necks).

Some PowerPoint slides are so ugly that they give audience members a headache just to look at it. When it comes to PowerPoint slides, less is more. The more you put on a slide, the less your audience will absorb, remember, or even pay attention.

It is bad enough to make people read words on a screen across the room because people are used to reading 12 to 20 inches away from their face, even if it is just a few words. To make people read whole paragraphs projected on a screen is an unpardonable sin. Your audience doesn't like it, and they aren't going to appreciate you subjecting them to this.

If you are going to use words on a PowerPoint screen (and I recommend you don't), be sure NOT to use complete sentences. Use no more than three bullet points, and each of these should have no more than three words.

It is crucial to avoid long sentences that wrap around from one side of the screen back to the beginning on the other side. Normally, if you are reading a wraparound sentence, like the preceding sentence on this page, it is easy on the eye. Your eye doesn't have to move more than six inches from the last word on one line at the right side to the first word on the next line on the left side. However, when you project sentences up on a 10, 20, or even a 30-foot screen, your wraparound sentences are forcing people to move their eyeballs 30 feet. At a subconscious level, that strikes most people as just too much work.

Keep it simple and pretty. Avoid the ugly slides filled with tons of words, boxes, arrows, and bullet points.

Free Your Hands

There is something about giving a PowerPoint Presentation that makes speakers want to fill their hands with lasers, pointers, remote controls, pens, notes, you name it. This is a major blunder. Anytime you are speaking, you want your hands to be as free as possible. The second your hand is holding something, it is less free to be expressive.

"But TJ, I need the laser to point out elements on my PowerPoint slides." If you need a laser to spotlight something on a slide, it usually means you have a bad slide. Your ideas should jump off the screen, not be so well hidden that you have to rescue them with a laser. Lasers are used primarily by people with cluttered, complicated slides. Don't be one of them.

Go back and look at the last PowerPoint presentation you gave and used a laser. Chances are, if something was so important that you had to stop and use a laser light to show it, then it is an element that deserves its own PowerPoint slide.

Confident people keep their hands free, and nervous people hold pens and notes as if they were life preservers keeping them from drowning. Naturally, you might be nervous when giving a PowerPoint, but that doesn't mean you have to let your audience know.

It's OK to use a remote control to advance your slides, but when you aren't using it, you should either place it on a table or lectern, or, if you have one of the thinner models, you may want to slide it into your pocket. Then, you can pull it out only when you need it and put it away immediately after changing slides.

It may seem trivial to obsess over a minor issue like holding a pen in your hand, but every element adds to the overall impression you leave with your audience. It is so simple to leave your hands free and yet so hard to recover if you give the audience the impression you are nervous or ill at ease.

The beauty of starting with your hands free during a PowerPoint presentation is that once you begin this way, you never have to think about this tip for the rest of your presentation. Instead, you can focus on communicating in the most authentic and memorable way possible.

Visuals Are Everything
In A Visual Medium

PowerPoint slides are an inherently visual medium. As such, it only takes one visual blunder to destroy your credibility. One spelling error projected on the big screen, and you are ruined.

For most PowerPoint presenters, spelling is not the problem. However, there are other visual imperfections that can be just as devastating to your reputation.

Too many presenters make last minute changes to their slides because Harry in the Chicago office emailed a new graph that has to be in the presentation in 10 minutes. Now you quickly insert it into your presentation. The only problem is that the way Harry laid out his page, a handful of his numbers now superimposes your logo graphic. The result is that your audience members can't make out the numbers, and your graphics look bad. You look like you are running amateur hour at the local middle school gymnasium.

There also needs to be consistent visual style throughout your slides. Stick to the same background color. Don't switch from bullet points to asterisks to stars. Use only one of these elements. Use one font style and size throughout, and make sure that the style is legible and the size is big enough to read.

Always preview your slides projected on the screen you will be using for the presentation. Many slides look great when you are 16 inches away from them on a computer screen. Although, when you are 20 feet away from them projected on a 15-foot screen, they may appear blurry, fuzzy, splotchy, or even chaotic.

Scrutinize your slides from every angle and perspective. Better yet, conduct some due diligence by asking another colleague to take a fresh look at them to give you feedback on any problems you might have missed.

In order to have your slides create the maximum positive impact, you must eliminate all mistakes and imperfections.

Where Were You When The Lights Went Out?

On August 14, 2003, I was conducting a presentation training workshop for a group of five executives from a Fortune 500 oil company. One of the first things I always stress during the morning of an all-day workshop that involves PowerPoint is the need to be prepared for any contingency.

"Always remember that you cannot count on technology. Your laptop could freeze. A bulb could burn out on your projector.

Someone could trip on a cord and send your projector or laptop to the ground and into a million pieces. Sometimes there is just bad karma."

I'm looking around the studio, and I see looks and nods of acknowledgement. Clearly, many of these things had happened before to the participants.

It's only 9:30 in the morning, and we have a full day of training ahead of us. I conclude this section by saying:

"Remember, you are never fully prepared to give a PowerPoint Presentation unless you can give the presentation without any slides at all. You never know, the electricity could go out, and you'll have to walk outside and deliver your presentation in the parking lot because there may be people who can only hear you that day. They are leaving for the airport in a few hours, and you will have no other opportunity to present to them.

Ultimately, the only thing you can truly count on is your ability to speak directly to people. If you are not prepared to give your PowerPoint without the PowerPoint, then you are not prepared."

We continued with the rest of the normal training day. This consisted of having each executive stand up, give his or her PowerPoint presentation while being videotaped and later critiqued.

Each executive gave a full speech three times, was critiqued after each, and showed improvement every time.

Now it is 4:00p.m.and time for each executive to give his or her final PowerPoint Presentation of the day. Just as the first executive stood up to speak, the lights went off.

"Darn, did we blow a fuse?" I thought.

No, the power was out everywhere in New York City and all across the Northeast and parts of Canada. The power wasn't restored for over 24 hours.

So what did we do?

The Media Training Worldwide TV studio has no windows; therefore, it is now pitch black.

"Everybody please remain seated." I said, not wanting anyone to trip and fall.

Fortunately, Media Training Worldwide publisher Greg Gerlovin quickly found a small flashlight. Using the small beam, we got up, found the door, got to the hallway, felt our way down the stairs, and walked out of the building.

Was that the end of the training day? No way.

Together, we walked half a block to Bryant Park, behind the New York City Public Library in Midtown Manhattan. There, we found six chairs and formed a semi-circle in the middle of the park. Then, each executive proceeded to stand up and give his or her PowerPoint Presentation, WITHOUT the benefit of slides of handouts.

The result? They each gave great presentations that were as good, or better, than their previous speeches using projectors and slides. Of course, they were only able to do this because they had just rehearsed and reviewed the same speech three times in one day. At 5:00 p.m., after they had all given their speeches, one of them said, "This was quite liberating. Now I know that if I prepare the right way, I don't have to worry about the stuff over which I have no control. As long as I'm prepared, I can communicate my ideas in any situation."

Exactly.

Fortunately, the quick thinking Gerlovin had rescued a six pack of beer from the TV studio refrigerator before our sudden exit, and now we could all enjoy some liquid refreshment on a hot summer day in the City.

And with that, the training day happily conclude.

Chapter 6:
Speaking Legends

Chapter 6:
Speaking Legends

Learn The Easy Way
From Other People's Mistakes

We've all been subjected to awful speakers—some are boring, others are sanctimonious, and a few are tedious. The one thing all of these rotten speakers have in common is this: listening to them is pure torture, and all you can think about is how you will never get the last thirty minutes of your life back.

Most of us tune out quickly once we are subjected to a lousy speaker. We pretend to take notes on our Palms, and we daydream about our summer vacations. Occasionally, we fall asleep.

The master communicator does none of these things while in an audience watching a bad speech. Instead, the master listens and watches the poor speaker AND watches the other audience members carefully. The master understands that the more you know about how and why other speakers lose their audience, the less likely you are to lose your own audience the next time you have to speak.

Only by watching and listening to dreadful speakers can you break down, step-by-step, exactly what are their mistakes. Once mistakes are isolated, it is easier to not repeat them.

The essential ingredient that master communicators must have is self-awareness. The masters must be able to see other people's blunders and acknowledge that they have made the same mistakes and are likely to do so again unless they remind themselves constantly not to repeat such mistakes.

For example, most of us have sat through countless business presentations from executives that are incredibly boring because the speaker quickly lists one abstract fact after another. The speaker races through 157 key developments that happened in his division during the last six months. Not a single example, story, anecdote, vignette, or case study is offered; rather, there's just a quick regurgitation of abstract bullet points.

We've all been there, and yet, most executives planning a presentation make the exact same blunder when creating and delivering their own speeches. Master communicators are not necessarily any smarter or harder working than average or boring speakers. The only difference is that they ask themselves, "Why would I want to subject someone to the same thing I hate myself?"

When given the option, I always choose to watch another speaker by standing at the front and far left or right side of the room. This allows for a clear and unobstructed view of the speaker and the rest of the audience without being distracting to them. From this

position, it is easy to see when a speaker is buried in notes, gives insufficient eye contact, or ignores whole sections of the room.

Take notes when you hear other people speak. They should include information on the subject matter as well as the speaker's presentation technique. Your notes may include entries such as this:

"Sally held everyone's attention brilliantly for the first five minutes as she gave us a blow-by-blow description of her battle with the account executive at the Acme Widget Company, but the second she launched into her slides, the energy went out of her voice and the room. Five minutes later, I noticed everyone was slouching and shifting in their chairs uncomfortably. After10 minutes of her slide presentation, I could swear I saw Dickinson nodding off and then catching himself and pretending to mask his snore with a throat clearing."

Everyone makes speaking mistakes. Master communicators reduce their mistakes by learning from your mistakes. You can too.

Focus Group Your Way
To Speaking Success

So, you have just finished what you think is one of your run-of-the mill presentations, but this time it is to a group twice the size of your normal speaking audience. After your speech, you are approached by three people.

Suzy says to you, "Great job on the presentation."

Sam says, "Nice speech today!"

Finally, Jim says (with a big smile), "I won't forget your speech today, that's for sure."

You smile to your colleagues, and you smile to yourself. You think, "Darn it, I AM good."

There is only one problem: your speech may have been horrible.

How can that be, you may ask, given all of the unsolicited praise? Unfortunately, praise like this is meaningless when it is so general and abstract.

Let's look again at the praise you received.

Suzy says, "Great job on the presentation." What she really means is "Please recommend me for that promotion to New York City."

Sam says, "Nice speech today!" What he is really saying is, "I deserve a raise."

And when Jim says, "I won't forget your speech today, that's for sure," he really means, "I won't forget it because you put me to sleep in the first 30 seconds, and I never heard it in the first place. Thanks for the time to catch up on my shuteye!"

When you receive praise from audience members immediately after you speak, here is what you should do if you are looking for meaningful feedback:

Say, "Thank you. What part of the speech stood out to you?" or "What part of the speech was most helpful?"

If the person complimenting you says something like, "Oh, everything about your speech was great," then you can assume your speech was a disaster and the person complimenting you is just giving you praise for other reasons, perhaps sympathy.

You should always probe audience members for what they remember in your speech. Which stories stick out in their minds?

How would they summarize your speech to a colleague who was not in attendance? This research is golden for a speaker, and it is FREE!

If you try out new material or a new story in a speech and nobody comments on it, maybe it wasn't so great after all. If everyone tells you after the speech that they loved the story you told near the end of your speech (almost as an afterthought) about the time you went to San Diego and pulled an all-nighter with your team in order to close the sale the next day, then maybe you should give that story more prominent placement in your next presentation.

Great speakers are often great because they use each and every single speech as an opportunity to get a free focus group on how to improve for their next speech. You can too, as long as you probe your audience members after you receive compliments.

Build Your Speaking Library

Picture one of your well-educated, articulate friends. He is a good writer, a skilled communicator, and a successful executive. When you go to this person's home, what do you expect to find? Somewhere in the house you will uncover a library or at least several shelves filled with books. There will probably be some works of literature, current bestsellers, religious or philosophical tracts, and perhaps some old college textbooks.

The point is, people who have to communicate by writing words usually surround themselves with books filled with printed words-for inspiration, examples, and, sometimes, just for good vibes. Yet, many of us (and this probably means you) don't surround ourselves with examples of our favorite speakers. This is a shame.

Who you consider to be a great speaker is a matter of personal taste. What is not debatable is the significant effect on your speaking if you regularly expose yourself to great speeches. So, if you admire Winston Churchill, buy or rent as many videos or CDs of his speeches that you can afford. Listen to them and watch them, just as you would reread a classic novel or replay a favorite movie. Note that it's not that you have to mimic Churchill's style in your next speech, but watching Churchill speak may inspire you to better prepare and rehearse for your next speech.

Maybe you don't like Churchill; then, get Jesse Jackson's speeches on CD or cassette. You will be surprised what you can find if you go to Amazon and type in the name of a famous person and then search under "DVD" or "CD."

If you are someone who hates politicians, don't worry. There are plenty of other good non-political speakers out there. Start by watching videos of your favorite standup comedians. Good comedians have many talents, but the main thing they all have in common is that they are great public speakers. You can learn a lot

by watching a Jerry Seinfeld or even a Carrot Top standup video, even if you never aspire to be funny.

Timing, gesturing, interacting with audiences, varying vocal tones, and capturing an audience's attention are all useful and relevant lessons you can learn by watching great standup comedians perform, as these skills are not limited solely to comedy.

The one thing most great writers have in common is that they regularly read a lot of good literature. While great speakers might not talk about it, they often share a secret habit: they surround themselves with video and audio examples of great speakers they admire.

So should you.

There Are No Little Speeches
Only Little Speakers

Recently, I asked a client of mine, the head of a foreign government, "How are you preparing for this upcoming speech?"

He replied, "It's nothing special, there will only be 100 people there. I wasn't going to prepare anything out of the ordinary."

I understood what he meant; as, for him, it was nothing special. He gives five speeches a day, usually to bigger or more influential audiences.

"But," I pointed out, "remember, for many of the people hearing you in the audience, this will be the first and last time they ever hear you, or ANY head of government, speak."

Every time you speak it is a chance to make a permanent impression (good or bad) on members of your audience. Obviously, no one who speaks frequently can give equal importance to every single speech. For example, a political leader who gives eight speeches a day can't practice each speech for two hours.

The easiest thing to do as a speaker is to dismiss smaller or less influential audiences. This, however, is a big mistake. A poor speech, no matter how short it may have been, is not soon to be

forgotten by people. The most common occurrence is that speakers give a boring and perfunctory speech—they sound like all of the other boring speakers. True, they don't harm their reputation, but they don't help it either; rather, they simply wasted everybody's time, including their own.

The best way to do well in your big, important speeches is to be great for the little and "unimportant" ones as well. Speaking well is a craft, and you either take it seriously or you don't. A great chef doesn't serve a sumptuous feast to one set of customers and then hand out SPAM and stale bread to other "less important" diners.

An important part of being a good speaker is conveying the following attitude to each and every audience: "You are important, and I am happy and lucky to have the opportunity to speak with you today!"

In the entertainment world, Bruce Springsteen is the master at this. He pours out every ounce of energy and passion in EVERY concert. Whether you hear him in New York, NY, or in Peoria, IL, you feel like Bruce is giving you something special, something extra tonight that he doesn't give just any audience. Are there nights Bruce would rather be home reading a good book and not have to jump around on stage? I'm sure there are, but he never lets the audience know it.

Whenever you are speaking, never give your audience any impression other than that you are incredibly excited and happy about speaking to them today.

Speak For As Long As
You Are Interesting

Clients often ask me, "TJ, how long should a speech be? Less than 20 minutes, right?"

I've read nearly every book ever written on public speaking and many of them purport to have scientific research that proves that if you speak for longer than 17 minutes and 13 seconds, you will completely lose your audience.

I take a different approach: Speak for as long as you have something really interesting to say.

If you are incredibly boring, a 30-second speech is too long. It is possible to put people to sleep in that short a period of time.

However, if you are interesting, your audience will hang on your every word—long past the supposed 20 or 30-minute threshold.

I've been to hundreds of Broadway shows over the years, and the most riveting show I ever saw was a one-man show called "21 DOG YEARS: DOING TIME @ AMAZON.COM" by Mike Daisey. It was in a small theater, a minimal set, and I knew nothing about the show. At the last minute, a couple of tickets fell my way, and I figured it would be a better use of time than watching another Seinfeld re-run.

I had low expectations. The show began, and out walked a thoroughly unimpressive, short, rumpled kid. I thought, "Wow, this is going to be a long evening, perhaps I can escape at intermission."

Then, this actor who I had never heard of opened his mouth. For the next 95 minutes, everything he said was interesting, engaging, insightful, and funny. When the show was over, I (along with the rest of the audience) was begging for the performer to go on another 95 minutes. It was the best show I had ever seen.

You may be thinking, "That's not relevant to me. I'm not an actor or an entertainer."

Fine, but it applies to anyone with an interesting message.

Regardless of how cheesy you think Anthony Robbin's infomercials are on late night TV, he is a captivating speaker. I have seen him

hold a crowd mesmerized from 9:00 a.m. until 11:00 p.m. with minimal breaks.

What's the real point here?

Don't worry so much about the exact length your presentation. Instead, spend time worrying about how you can make your presentation so interesting and memorable that people are talking about you for days, weeks, even months later.

Learn from Friend And Foe Alike

One thing that separates good communicators from great communicators is that the great ones are constantly on the prowl for new ideas on how to improve their style, technique, and delivery process—and they don't care where they get their ideas. Great communicators learn how to differentiate style from substance. This allows them to listen to any speaker in person or through the media and simultaneously judge them on content and form.

Most people don't do this. The average person listens or watches a speaker and judges only from the perspective of content. What was the message? At a less than fully conscious level, most of us judge whether we like someone and if they make us feel comfortable, but

that's it. If we don't like someone's message, we tend to write him off as a bad person or not worthy of hearing.

The result?

Liberal Democrats don't listen to Rush Limbaugh, and they refuse to learn anything about his communication strengths because they don't like his conservative message.

Conservative Republicans can't watch Bill Clinton on a TV screen for more than 20 seconds without shouting at the screen and turning the channel because they don't like him personally. Many moderates turn off anyone they perceive to have strong opinions of any persuasion.

All three groups are missing out on tremendous learning opportunities.

The master communicator watches and listens to the widest array of speakers, politicians, and commentators. He or she then borrows, mixes, and matches the best techniques from others into his or her own future speeches.

The liberal master communicator professional will listen to Rush Limbaugh for hours and marvel at his skill at maintaining a conversational tone of voice, sounding spontaneous, and inserting

humor and his sheer cleverness. The liberal professional learns from Limbaugh and doesn't turn it off the second a disagreeable opinion is uttered.

The conservative master communicator will watch Bill Clinton speak every time the opportunity presents itself. The conservative professional revels in the mastery of Clinton's superb eye contact, ability to project warmth and empathy, and dazzling level of articulateness that allows him to speak in flawlessly constructed sentences and paragraphs for long periods of time. The conservative communication professional doesn't tune out Clinton just because of a distaste for his personality.

It's not that high level communicators are constantly trying to imitate every other great speaker they see—the goal is not to mimic or be an impressionist. Rather, by constantly making yourself aware of how other people communicate well, you heighten your awareness of your strengths and weaknesses. Occasionally, master communicators may add a new element to their presentation style, but they never make radical changes to the way they speak or imitate a famous speaker.

If you want to become a great communicator, you must develop the practice of using both of your ears at the same time for different purposes. Use your left ear to hear the content and message. Use

your right ear (and eyes) to observe to the style, technique, and form of the speaker.

This way, you will learn from every speaker —even if it is learning what NOT to do.

Paul Harvey............Good Day!

The great communicator is always on the lookout for good role models. One of the best you could ever find is on a radio dial near you: national news commentator Paul Harvey. Harvey has been broadcasting daily since, roughly, 1890. He's now approximately 157 years old. Yet, he sounds the same as he did 10, 20, even 40 years ago. (If you have never heard of Paul Harvey, try to find the top rated news and talk AM radio station in your town. Harvey does four daily news, comment, and feature segments of varying lengths.)

Harvey is an absolute master at using the full range of his voice and pauses to maximum advantage (It's quite an advantage—he makes tens of millions of dollars a year!). Harvey always has perfect delivery. He sounds conversational, and his voice ranges high, low, and everything in between. If he's amused, his voice registers amusement. When he finds something contemptuous, you feel it instantly in his voice. You can pull a 60-second excerpt from any

part of Harvey's broadcast and feel like you are on a rollercoaster— the ups and downs in his voice never sound contrived and always make you feel like you are on an interesting journey.

Try listening to a five-minute segment from Harvey and contrasting that with a five-minute segment from a typical businessperson's speech. (It will not be a pretty comparison). You will notice several differences. The average businessperson will get about twice as many words out during those five minutes than Harvey. But, and this is an important but, you will find that an hour later, you will remember nothing from the businessperson's speech and yet many things from Harvey's broadcast.

In addition to using the entire range of his voice for maximum expressive affect, Harvey is also the master of doing nothing. That's right, nothing (i.e., pausing), while talking. Harvey knows that the way to put emphasis on something is to pause. The way to build drama is to pause. The way to build anticipation is to pause. The way to get your audience to visualize is to pause. The way to get your audience to reflect is to pause. The way to sound a thousand times more comfortable, confident, and relaxed than every other speaker is to pause.

Harvey even has a signature pause in his closing. According to Harvey, early in his career, he simply ran out of enough material for a tightly timed broadcast segment. He finished his script, and then

he said nothing for several seconds until he concluded with "Good day!" And, somehow, it worked, and he kept doing it. Now, tens of thousands of broadcasts later, Harvey ends his commentaries with the signature:

"Paul Harvey…(pause for several seconds)…Good Day!"

The Reagan Rhetorical Legacy

Ronald Reagan was called "The Great Communicator." Was it because he was just a natural? Or, was it because he was a trained actor?

No and no. Although some of his background as an actor did help him during these times, Reagan simply understood that a speech isn't about the speaker, it's about the audience. He didn't speak to entertain himself; instead, he spoke to communicate with his audience.

What does this mean as a practical matter? Reagan gave essentially the same speech all across the country from 1964 when he became a paid spokesman for General Electric until he got elected President in 1980. Most people can't stand the idea of repeating themselves for two days, much less 16 years.

But, Reagan understood human nature--specifically that you reach humans not just by facts but through the personal and emotional level. That's why he instructed his staff to never have him speak for more than two minutes without mentioning a real human being, preferably as part of a story. Reagan knew that most people comprehend the world through stories, not cold abstractions. Reagan supporters loved his stories about "Morning in America," while his detractors were outraged at his riffs on "Welfare queens who drive Cadillacs," but no one ever doubted that Reagan's stories where true reflections of his core beliefs.

Regan was the first president to have individuals stand in the gallery during the State of the Union Address. It was a brilliant move to personalize an important, abstract message point and good for the TV cameras.

Reagan was a serious student of rhetoric. While he had an appreciation for classical rhetorical devises, even those used by Kennedy ("Ask not what your country can do for you..."), Reagan concluded that in the modern television age, these could make a political leader look and sound stilted and overly formal. Reagan was quick to scratch out and edit any fancy flourishes that his speechwriters occasionally tried to insert into White House speeches. Reagan believed that he must maintain a conversational tone in his speech and his sentence structure anytime he was speaking. This is also why Reagan never yelled while giving a

speech. He understood that in the age of microphones and camera close-ups, yelling was unnecessary and even counterproductive, a lesson that Al Gore has never learned.

While Reagan was not always perfectly smooth in unscripted press conference situations, he had a keen appreciation for the sound bite. He knew what the press wanted, he knew his message, and he knew how to package one for the other.

"Tear down that wall, Mr. Gorbachev!"

That classic sound bite had action, emotion, attacks, and was highly personal—all the essential elements needed to make reporters swoon—and it worked.

Reagan understood that any presentation he gave started well before he opened his mouth. He gave intense scrutiny to every element of his visual presentation. If you look at old footage of Reagan during his presidency, you will be hard pressed to ever find a shot of him speaking or walking to a lectern with his suit jacket un-buttoned. Nor will you find a shot of him buttoning his jacket. These are seemingly minor elements, but they play a part in creating the mystique of a presenter. Reagan understood that you don't let the audience backstage see any aspects of the preparation—even for as mundane an act as buttoning your jacket.

As Reagan aged, he shunned the face-lifts popular with most of his Hollywood colleagues. As his neck sacked and became more wrinkled, Reagan compensated by having his shirt collar slightly too large by normal standards. By never having the shirt collar tight around his neck, it took attention away from the one weakness in his physical appearance.

Reagan brought an extraordinary discipline to the White House communications process. He would require that all major speeches be finished one week before they were to be delivered, a discipline not followed by any of his successors. This would allow him time to personally make many edits and changes and to practice.

Perhaps the biggest mistaken notion about Reagan as a communicator is that he was such a natural that he could just pick up a script and deliver it well on a first reading. Reagan knew that communicating well was a function of hard work. For every major speech, especially State of the Union addresses, he would take the final text up to his private study in the personal quarters of the White House and read the words out loud for hours every night for the entire week prior to the presentation. Then, he would spend the day before a big speech in a formal rehearsal that included videotaping with feedback and critique from his media and communications advisors.

By the time Reagan was actually reading his speech from the TelePrompTer in front of the American people on national TV, he was so comfortable with the words that he could make them his own and inject them with feeling. Reagan clearly understood that the words themselves are 7 percent of the total impression a speaker leaves on an audience. The rest of the message comes from the speaker's voice, inflections, facial expressions, and body language. He clearly understood he was not simply a deliverer of words.

Of course, when you are president, not every speech is as important as the State of the Union. A president must give a dozen speeches a week or more. In this case, most Presidents, or for that matter, most other speakers rely on reading notes in front of audiences.

For most speakers, reading from notes is a painful, boring experience for an audience (think of Gerald Ford stumbling his way through a prepared statement), but Reagan knew all of the tricks to this communications process as well.

Reagan read many of his speeches, but he used a different technique than most speakers: He would glance down at the script, but he would not move his head. He'd look down and see his first line, but would not read it aloud. He would wait until he was looking directly at audience members before he would say the line; now, he had internalized it and made it sound personal. After saying his line, he would pause to let his audience reflect upon it. While the audience

was reflecting, Reagan had time to quickly glance down to see what the next line was in his speech.

This technique takes some practice and requires spacing your speech differently on the page, but the rewards are immense. Reagan's audiences felt mesmerized by him, even when he was reading perfunctory remarks off of note cards.

Finally, Reagan's career demonstrates the potential for ONE speech to make an entire career. Of course Regan had a cachet as a "B" level actor in the 40s and 50s, but by the early 60s, his Hollywood career was over. It was his electrifying speech on behalf of Barry Goldwater at the 1964 Republican convention that propelled him into the California governor's race in 1966 and ultimately to the presidency.

While Theodore Roosevelt coined the term "Bully Pulpit" in describing the power of being in the Oval Office, Reagan did more to focus on and harness the communications power of the presidency than any leader who served before or after him.

Senator John Kerry guaranteed the Democratic nomination with his nine of 10 wins on Super Tuesday. Moreover, much has been made of his speaking style, as it's been called "aloof," "stiff," and "elite."

Why is this?

Kerry uses an extraordinarily formal, pre-television style of speaking. He clutters his speeches with lots of bombastic phrases such as "and I say to you, my fellow Americans..."

What does that phrase mean? Nothing. We know he is "saying" something because words are coming out of his mouth. We know he is talking to "fellow Americans" because his fellow citizens of Portugal can't vote for him.

It is true that President John Kennedy also used lots of these essentially meaningless phrases. But 44 years ago when Kennedy was on the scene, everyone still used flowery, formal written speeches. All Kennedy had to do was show up without a five o'clock shadow, smile, show a clean shirt, and he was proclaimed a TV God. Kerry is not so lucky.

Mike Luckovich, a syndicated cartoonist, sums up Kerry's problem with a recent cartoon. Kerry is speaking at a rally in South Carolina and says in the cartoon balloon, "National Association of stock car auto racing aficionados, I beseech you, support me!"

Behind Kerry is one aide saying to another, "I keep telling him, call 'em 'NASCAR fans.'"

We are a "Today Show" nation where the highest paid and most respected communicators talk in a conversational, personal style. Voters and viewers tend to find any other style grating and phony.

President Bush has numerous weakness and flaws as a public speaker. However, he does speak in a conversational manner most of the time, which made him less of an annoying speaker than Al Gore four years ago.

Quick, name the last time the best communicator of the two presidential candidates actually lost?

The Dean Scream

A 2004 New York Times story suggests that former Vermont Governor Howard Dean's shrieking or yelling sound bite after the Iowa caucuses will be the new standard for bad sound bites by which all future poor sound bites will be judged.

But did it kill his candidacy? Dean's campaign had been hemorrhaging for weeks, and after the dismal third place finish in Iowa, most political observers concluded the Dean campaign was headed to a quick death. This was the consensus before the yell.

After the yell?

It was no longer a hemorrhage. It had the effect of driving a stake through his heart, quickly putting the corpse in a body bag, then a cheap coffin, and then out to the cemetery in the poor part of town where poor Howard's body was buried without so much as a grave maker.

The unanswerable question is this: What would have happened to Dean if he had won the Iowa Caucus and then emitted the yell?

The real lesson for Dean and other politicians and public figures is the following: If you are talking to a group of people and there is a TV camera in the room, the most important conversation you are having is with viewers at home who are watching in their living rooms and bedroom.

With a speech in a room full of people, context is everything. Dean was passionately and energetically communicating with a room full of enthusiastic supporters the night of the yowl. The room was small, the crowd large, and the noise level loud. To anyone in the room hearing Dean that night, the governor sounded great. Not only did people there not think that he had blundered or sounded strange, they though that this was yet another great example of why they believed he was a charismatic leader. Dean simply appeared passionate and full of conviction—exactly what the crowd wanted.

So, why did anyone who saw Dean on TV come away with the belief that Dean is an insane, deranged, unhinged, disturbed individual whose next home should be in a psychiatric ward instead of Pennsylvania Avenue?

There are two reasons--one technical and one contextual.

Dean was using a unidirectional microphone, meaning the mic only picked up sound in one direction--from his mouth. That means the microphone didn't pick up the sound from the rest of the screaming and cheering crowd. Dean had to yell simply to be heard by the crowd and to hear himself. None of that is apparent when you see a close-up of him on TV, seemingly yelling for no reason.

If Dean only had the good fortune of using a multidirectional microphone, the sound of the crowd would have leveled out his own noises. No sound bite. No Jay Leno. No David Letterman. No Diane Sawyer.

If you see a crowd of people yelling and screaming at a football game, nothing looks or sounds odd or out of place. But, if you were to edit out the entire crowd and everyone else's yelling and showed just yourself jumping up and down yelling and screaming on TV, everyone would think you had gone nuts.

Context is everything. When you are speaking to people live in a room, you have the time and ability to start slow, explain things, give detail, show a range of emotion, and then climax in the end with some strong finish. Being slow and understated one minute and a little bit "hot" somewhere in your speech can make you a quite engaging speaker.

Unfortunately, if you are captured for television, you lose control of the context. Every sentence, every phrase, or in Dean's case, every bizarre sound out of is captured and can be replayed in a vacuum. A little emotion in a speech is like a nice seasoning in a good meal—necessary, but due to the context-destroying power of TV, it's as though you are forced to eat a meal that is nothing but a pound of fresh ground pepper on an empty plate—not tasty or filling but gives you heartburn.

Pundits like to make fun of boring and bland career politicians like Dick Gephardt. The reality is, however, that you don't get to be a career politician without being cautious around the TV camera. It only takes one "hot" moment to end your career.

The Evolution Of Bush,

The Speaker

Regardless of what you think of President George W. Bush's policies or personality, he has clearly evolved as a public speaker during the last four years. Bush is still quite shaky in press conference and TV interview situations, but he has improved dramatically in his prepared speeches.

When Bush first started running for President in 1999 and early 2000, he often raced through his speeches, never pausing, tripping over words in the process and robbing them of any emotion. He took these flaws into the Oval Office his first year. He also used the TelePrompTer poorly. He committed the beginner's blunder of reading too quickly, not varying speed, and not moving his head enough.

The turning point for Bush's presidency was after 9-11 when he stood atop the rubble with a megaphone and shouted down, "I hear you, and all of America hears you...." It was unscripted; therefore, it sounded conversational, emotional, and real. It helped Bush connect with many citizens.

Another turning point came for Bush during the 2004 campaign. Bush gave the same campaign speech at many locations around the country, so Bush developed a comfort with the content to the point

where he didn't feel he had to read it. The President was then able to speak in a more conversational manner. Specifically, he put in a lot more pauses, and he sometimes spoke faster, sometimes slower, sometimes louder, and sometimes softer because this is what all good speakers do regularly.

It's unlikely that Bush will ever be compared favorably to Reagan or Clinton as a speaker, but he has shown that it is possible for anyone to improve basic speaking skills through practice and the use of simple techniques like pausing more frequently.

Chapter 7:
Question And Answer

Chapter 7:
Question And Answer

The Question Of Questions

Question time is a highly valuable part of any presentation, and it's one that many speakers flub. For starters, many presenters don't plan enough time for questions from the audience. This occurs for two main reasons: One, if the speaker is allotted an hour for a presentation, he or she writes an hour's worth of material because of the fear of running short. Second, the speaker writes material or plans a PowerPoint that seemingly runs only 30 minutes, but the difference between practicing in your head versus saying it out loud in front of a real audience is very different. It will take much longer actually speaking it than reading it to yourself. Once again, there is no time left for questions.

This is a huge mistake. You want to give people plenty of time to ask you questions. People's brains absorb information differently. What may seem perfectly clear to you may be cloudy to half your audience. Your answers to their questions can clarify your content.

It's not bad if you do run short occasionally. If you are allotted an hour and you speak for 35 minutes and have 10 minutes of questions, is anyone really going to complain that you didn't fill the full hour? Of course not. You are the hero of the day.

It is important for the speaker to fully understand what is going on when an audience member asks a question. A question means the audience member is (1) listening to you, (2) trying to understand you, (3) trying to determine personal relevance to the material at hand, and (4) is engaged in the moment; after all, you can't be a sleeping audience member if you are talking.

In other words, it is GREAT when audience members ask you questions. Don't ever assume questions mean you were less than wonderful as a speaker or that the audience is questioning your authority or legitimacy.

You should always want questions from your audience.

Clients often ask me, "Should I let audience members interrupt my presentation or hold all questions until the end?"

This requires a judgment call based on three factors:
1. Size of the audience.
2. Complexity of the subject matter.
3. Strictness of your time limits for your presentation.

If you are speaking to an audience of more than 20 people, it gets too distracting to allow audience members to interrupt at any point. However if you are talking to fewer than 20 people, I would

strongly encourage the audience to ask questions at any time during the presentation. It is much more interesting for your audience if they can participate, be a part of the dialogue, and have questions answered according to the way their brain works instead of yours. For small groups (most presentations are given to small groups), it is less boring for audience members to be able to ask questions instantly. Remember, no audience member is falling asleep if he or she is asking you a pertinent question. Furthermore, you will come across as much more polished, confident, and unscripted if you take questions throughout your presentation.

There are times when someone asks a question and it is impossible to answer it without having to cover a series of other concepts that you are going to cover later in the presentation. For example, sometimes I have clients I am training for media interviews ask me early in a training session how to speak in quotable sound bites. I can't teach them about sound bites until I've spent at least two hours teaching them how to create a media message and how to answer reporters' questions. So, in this case, I let the questioner know that we will get to that later and that I cannot go into it just yet because of the complexity. Many other times I am asked questions regarding material I wasn't going to cover until later in the training, but it is a topic that can be easily explained in a minute. In that case, I answer the question immediately and fully. This way, I satisfy the questioner and put my own agenda secondary.

The final issue is time. There are situations when you are given a precise 15-minute window to give a presentation and not a second more. In these cases, you may want to hold questions until the end to make sure you have gotten your core message delivered. You don't want to get sidetracked with irrelevant questions for 10 minutes and then have to skim over your most important content.

Even in these time-controlled situations, I would never automatically hold all questions to the end of the presentation. If you are two minutes into a presentation for a new client prospect and a key decision maker in the audience asks a very direct question, I would answer it right away and then get back to your planned presentation.

Finally, I am often asked, "What do you do if there are no questions after your presentation?"

It may be that you were so clear and convincing that no one has any questions, but the more likely scenario is that your audience members are still processing your speech. It is always good to plan for these situations. Try to have at least one interesting or important point to share with your audience during question time. After you have announced that you will take questions, calmly wait several beats. Never convey that you are concerned or embarrassed that there are no questions. If no one speaks, then smile and say, "Before I came up here today I was asked...." Then, state an interesting

question you have been asked in the past and give a good answer to it. (You are being truthful even if someone asked you the question six months earlier because you are saying it was asked before you came up here, not how long before).

That should prime the pump for more people to ask questions.

Ask Questions, Don't Write Questions

Many speakers and organizers of presentations request that people in their audience submit questions, sometimes even in advance of the presentation. This is disastrous for the following reasons:

1. Forcing your audience to write down their questions robs them of spontaneity.

2. Having the questions written means you must now read them. It is boring for your audience to hear you read, and you lose eye contact with your audience when you are reading.

3. Many people don't like to write or are simply not confident in their grammar. In this case, they will refuse to write a question, and you lose the opportunity to answer.

4. Some people have bad handwriting, and it would be embarrassing for you and them if you tried to read a question but couldn't comprehend what it said.

5. Many in your audience will assume you are throwing away tough questions, even if you aren't.

6. Some in your audience will assume you are not tough or confident enough to directly face people.

7. If you force people to submit questions before the presentation is finished, you run the risk of having questions that were already dealt with during the speech.

8. If people have to write the questions down before the speech is concluded, they won't be able to reflect on the entire message and then ask thoughtful questions based on their own conclusions, hence the questions will be superficial.

9. Occasionally, the host or organizer uses the reading of questions as an opportunity to steal the limelight, thus detracting from the speaker.

10. Finally, there is something reminiscent of old Soviet Union control-focused bureaucracy when you ask people to write questions in advance.

Don't do it.

Bad Speech – Great Q & A Session

One thing I hear all of the time from my presentation-training clients is, "I'm not great at the prepared section of my speech, but I feel I truly excel during the question and answer session. I feel more comfortable, and people tell me that I seem exceptionally strong and convincing during question time."

This is a common speaker fallacy. Ideally, you are no better at answering questions after a speech than you are at giving your prepared speech because you are EQUALLY excellent during both parts of the presentation. There is nothing inherently harder or easier about answering questions or delivering the structured part of your speech. It is not as though someone in the audience is requiring you to deliver the first half of your speech with a mouth full of marbles and then you are allowed to spit them out before taking questions.

All of the conditions are exactly the same in the room. This means that anything you do well when you are answering questions can be replicated during the prepared part of your speech.

Once I explain this, the typical response is, "but it's much easier during the question and answer session because I'm not dealing with a script, and I can give examples, and it's a chance to be more conversational."

In this case I respond, "EXACTLY! Now do that all the time."

These are the same elements you should strive to incorporate into every aspect of your presentation from the moment you stand up, through your prepared presentation and the Q&A session, until you sit back down.

What kills many speakers' effectiveness during the prepared portion of their speech is an overly long, elaborate, and abstract outline that features one mind-numbing fact after another. It is impossible to talk in a conversational way while using such a poor speech structure.

The simplest way to make the prepared part of your speech as strong and comfortable as the Q&A portion is to simply steal the format of the Q&A session and use it in your prepared speech. Rather than write out your speech in the traditional manner, write out the 10 or 20 questions you think your audience would want to ask you about the subject if you were having a one-on-one conversation with a single audience member. Further, it's OK to literally speak out the question to your audience during the speech and then answer your own question, using examples, stories, and facts. Then, in a conversational way, move to the next question.

The focus for any presenter who wishes to improve should be to isolate examples of when he or she does particularly well in any

speaking opportunity. Once you have identified your best situation (for example: speaking to small groups vs. large, standing versus sitting), the task is now to identify the precise elements of what you are doing that makes you do well in this format. Then, the trick is to force yourself to do that exact thing in every speaking environment, no matter how many factors have changed. For example, if you always answer questions with real life examples and stories, but when giving so-called formal speeches, you always speak at the abstract-30,000 feet- level, then you have a problem. Fortunately, this is a problem with an easy solution that does not require learning difficult new skills. Instead, it just requires you to do what works well for you when speaking one-on-one, providing content with lots of personal examples that relate to you and your audience members.

The real danger of speaking in a dull, flat, and boring manner during your prepared presentation and then being great in the Q&A session is that most of your audience will have tuned out or fallen asleep before you get to question time. Then, it won't matter how brilliant you are during that portion. Your audience is gone for good, and they probably won't have any questions for you anyway.

Chapter 8:
I'm Dying Up Here

Chapter 8:
I'm Dying Up Here

Coping With Extreme Fear

What do you do if you have an extreme case of public speaking Heebie-Jeebies? What if you are beyond the normal fear level when it comes to speaking in public or in front of a TV camera? Sure, other people joke about preferring a root canal or being in a casket over giving a public speech, but you REALLY mean it.

What do you do if you have read all of my tips, followed all of my suggestions, read every book on the subject of speaking in public, and you are still scared out of your mind?

What do you do if you start to perspire so much you look like Albert Brooks in Broadcast News? What if you sweat so much from your hands that a pool of perspiration forms on the floor in front of you?

Well, extreme situations sometimes require extreme solutions. Please realize that the following recommendations I am giving are not for the average bashful speaker; conversely, these tips are for the bottom .01 percent of speakers who face paralysis at the thought of speaking to more than two people.

1. Ask your doctor to prescribe a Beta-blocker. This drug is not addictive and won't make you high, but it will keep you from getting tensed up. Many star performers have occasionally used it. The drawback is that you may have to speak in the future, and you won't always have immediate access to the drug, then you will be twice as nervous.

2. Have your dermatologist inject your underarms and hands with Botox. This will greatly reduce excessive perspiring. Yes, it may seem extreme to inject botulism from cows into your body, but at least it won't make you look Frankensteinian like many people do who inject Botox into their faces once too often. The drawback here is that you have to get more injections every six months in order to keep the effect.

3. You are going to think I'm kidding here, but I'm not. If you suffer from extreme sweating, you can actually apply clear antiperspirant directly to your forehead. This will minimize your visible sweating. Just make sure you don't leave any shiny residue. Either blend it in or cover it up with facial powder before you go on TV or appear before a crowd.

You must find what works for you to minimize your nerves, but whatever you do, don't drink alcohol to reduce your nerves. Liquor will make you sweat more and increase the odds that you lose your train of thought.

You Can Get A Second Chance
To Make A Great Impression

Of course you never want to go into a presentation opportunity thinking, "OK, I'll be lousy here because I can always do better next time." That's highly counterproductive. However, one bad speech or even a string of poor presentations will not kill you as long as you hone your skills and start to deliver great presentations. Your peers, colleagues in your company, and your industry will start to think of you as a great communicator in a short period of time if you start giving excellent presentations, no matter how many lackluster speeches you've given in the past.

By all accounts, then-Governor Bill Clinton flubbed his keynote address at the 1988 Democratic Convention in Atlanta. He was way too long, lost his audience, and was literally booed. The only time he brought about a cheer was when he said "and in conclusion." That brought the house down—not exactly what a speaker is hoping for out of his presentation. Clinton didn't wait long to rehabilitate his image. He went on the Today Show the very next morning to make fun of himself and to reposition himself as a more engaging speaker. Over time and with many well-delivered speeches, even Clinton's worst enemies (he did have a few, didn't he?) forgot his debacle of '88.

If you ask Americans who were some of the greatest speakers of the 20th century, President John F Kennedy makes the top 10 on any list, but he was not always considered a good communicator. As late as the mid-50s when Kennedy was a Senator, he was known as a lackluster speaker who came across as shy, awkward, lacking in vigor, and not that interesting. I've had Democratic activists who heard Kennedy speak to small political clubs in New York City tell me, "Kennedy came across like any other run of the mill city council candidate—he was mediocre at best."

But, Kennedy changed. He practiced. He improved.

You can too.

Screwing Up While Nobody Notices

Great speakers and average speakers both make frequent mistakes when they speak. Both groups occasionally botch a word. Both types of speakers occasionally forget a word. Average and poor speakers have their minds go totally blank from time to time in front of audiences, and this happens to great speakers too.

So, why does one speaker gain the reputation for eloquence and poise while the other speaker who makes the same number of blunders develops the reputation for mediocrity?

The difference lies not in the number of mistakes made, but in how they react to the mistakes.

The mediocre speaker will stumble over a word, then stop and wince, or create a look of horror on his or her face. The outstanding speaker will make a mistake, but keep going while wearing a pleasant smile.

The reality is that the audience didn't catch the mistake of either speaker. But the audience did notice how the first speaker reacted to the mistake. The grimace, the upward eye roll, or the look of embarrassment was immediately felt by the audience. Now the audience realizes something went wrong. They are either trying to figure out what went wrong or they are feeling sympathy for you, neither of which you want as a speaker.

There is a fundamental difference between hearing words spoken versus reading words on a piece of paper—and all great speakers know this. If you use an incorrect word, or switch the proper order, or don't use perfect grammar in written text, 95 percent of your readers will immediately detect your mistakes and think poorly of you. However, if you make those same mistakes while speaking, 95 percent of your audience will not be able to hear your mistake.

This is not a license to be sloppy or make mistakes on purpose. However, it is crucial for speakers to understand the difference in how audiences process information when they are hearing you speak rather than reading.

The vast majority of the time, if you don't telegraph your mistakes after the fact to your audience, they won't catch them.

So, what if your mind goes blank in the middle of a presentation? The amateur speaker plasters a terrified look on his face, starts to sweat, gasps, and mutters some apology like, "Oh my God, my mind just went blank. Please forgive me."

Not impressive at all.

What does the professional speaker do when her mind goes blank in the middle of a speech? She simply stops, looks out to a different person in the audience, and pauses. She projects a serene look of confidence that suggests, "I just gave you such an important insight that I am now going to do you the favor of having a few seconds to reflect on it." The skilled speaker makes it seem like the pause was on purpose, even though it wasn't. Now the speaker can figure out something else to say without looking flustered. If all else fails, you can always say, "so what does this really mean to you?" and then cover what you just mentioned in a slightly different way.

The skilled speaker doesn't panic because she also realizes that the audience does not have the outline of the speech; therefore, they do not realize she has blanked out or forgotten her place. Thus, if she picks up from a different point in the outline, it's not going to matter to the audience as long as it is presented in an interesting and understandable manner.

Obviously, you can't use this crutch repeatedly throughout a speech, but every once in a while you can get away with it.

So, keep that grimace to yourself.

Chapter 9:
Other Problems

Chapter 9:
Other Problems

How Do You Keep From Going Stale?

Many observers of the John Edwards for President campaign marveled at how well the candidate repeatedly delivered his same stump speech with no variation. His pitch, timing, pauses, and emotional impact were flawless every time. To the audience to which he was speaking, he seemed as fresh as if he were having a spontaneous conversation with them for the first time.

How did he do it?

Further, how can you do it if you are forced to give the same canned speech to employees, prospects, or clients time after time?

If you've ever felt this way, you are not alone. One of my clients just asked me the following question:

"When you've done a speech a lot of times--to the point the jokes and the timing are so consistent--how do you keep from putting yourself into a trance? Sometimes I feel like I am hearing myself instead of just speaking?"

There are several ways of handling this problem.

1. Put in moments of planned spontaneity, where you appear to be searching for a word or next phrase. A pause that has the look and feel of being unplanned will keep you from going into a trance.

2. Change your speech a little each time. For example, drop a section that doesn't seem to be memorable and add a new story in its place. Great speakers use each audience as a focus group to make the next speech a little better.

3. Focus on your audience, not whether it is interesting to you. Don't be selfish. The speech isn't for you, and your audience hasn't heard it as many times as you, if at all.

4. How do you keep from going into a trance when someone asks you how you met your husband or wife? If you are married, you have to talk about that fairly often, right?

5. Remember, Ronald Reagan gave the same speech for General Electric around the country from 1964 to 1980, and look where he ended up.

One of my friends used to work for TV talk show host Larry King and had to hear him give speeches to convention audiences quite frequently. So, I asked him, "Jim, how was Larry as a speaker?"

Jim said, "It was awful, so boring to listen to. I had to hear the same darn stories over and over again."

And I asked Jim, "How did the audiences respond."

Jim replied, "The response was always the same. The audiences laughed, cried, cheered, and then gave him a standing ovation. They loved him."

What Larry King understands is that his speech isn't about his enjoyment, even though the speech is about him. The speech is about what an audience gets by hearing you for the first time on this subject.

When, Not If, You Bomb

If you speak long and often enough, you will occasionally bomb a speech. The important thing is to learn from your mistakes and make yourself even stronger for your next presentation.

Early in my career, I had been booked to give a speech at a Manhattan political club. It was an election year and the political club's party candidate was the current U.S. President running for re-election. I assumed--as it turns out incorrectly--that members of a particular political party would want the incumbent of their own party to be re-elected.

Big mistake.

This being Manhattan, everything and everyone is a bit, shall we say, different (I can say this now because I have lived here for a decade). Members of this political club did not find the President from their own political party to be ideologically pure enough (This is something you will find in almost any organization based in New York City).

I gave a speech similar to many presentations I had given around the country. I started by making some jokes about members of the other party. These usual laugh-getters were met with stony faces. Next, I gave a detailed strategy on how club members could help their party's nominee by calling talk radio shows, writing letters to the editor, appearing as guests on TV programs, and other media strategies. This was met with looks of pure bewilderment.

With much grumbling in the audience, my speech finally stumbled to an ending.

"Great," I thought, "Now the questions and answers can make up for lost time."

Sure enough the first question comes.

"Young man, how long have you lived in Manhattan, and what makes you think you could possibly have anything intelligent to tell us?"

Gulp.

This was going to be a long night.

Fortunately, my audience had such contempt for me that they all quickly left the building.

As I was walking home in a snowstorm on that April Fool's day, I asked myself, "Where did I go wrong?"

Then, I realized that I had made the classic blunder of assuming a one-size-fits-all style for my speech. I hadn't done enough homework to find out about the particular concerns of this audience. I hadn't gotten to the event early enough to talk to members one-on-one to find out what they were thinking. I didn't adjust quickly enough once I was making the speech. In short, I made about every mistake a speaker could make.

So, was the lesson to avoid all public speaking in the future?

No. The lesson was to find some more speaking gigs quickly and to wow my next set of audiences thoroughly. That's what I did, and that's what you can do after your next bomb.

The key is, don't think of your speech as a bomb, think of it merely as a rough draft for your next great speech.

Beware The Over-Reaction Into
One Size Fits All

If both of your parents were alcoholics who beat you as a small child, you may have become traumatized to the point where you got scared being around any adult because you assumed an abusive beating was about to occur. Sadly, many business presenters have been similarly traumatized by the parent figure (the boss) that is abusive during an employee's presentations.

Of course, most bosses don't actually beat their employees while the underlings are giving presentations. No, the form of abuse is strictly verbal and psychological.

The boss says something like this when the employee is trying to give a report on everything that has happened in her department the last three months:

"Faster, faster, get to the point! I don't have all day!"

The employee is now reduced to reading numbers and bullet points off of a script or a PowerPoint chart in a machine gun fashion. The boss isn't really interested in hearing a speech or learning anything from the employee's presentation. He is the sort of person who absorbs information by reading. He is reading the PowerPoint slides

or handouts. The employee is just there to answer questions. The "presentation" is a formality that has nothing to do with any communication process.

If the boss who signs your paycheck tells you to speak faster and faster while covering 179 bullet points in 3.2 minutes, then by all means, do it. A good speaker gives the audience what it wants, and in this case, the audience of one wants you quickly rattling off facts.

Here is where the problem occurs. Just as the child of abusive alcoholic parents generalizes that all adults are dangerous and should be avoided, the speaker with this sort of boss generalizes that all speeches should be delivered quickly by dishing out many facts and numbers in the shortest amount of time possible.

This may "work" for your boss in the sense that that is what he wants and it makes him satisfied, but using this method of presenting to colleagues, customers, clients, employees, prospects, or the public at large is a prescription for one thing only:

A FAILURE TO COMMUNICATE

One size does not fit all when it comes to presenting to different audiences, but if you are speaking in the manner described above, you are assured of losing, boring, and confusing them. To 99.99 percent of the world, there is nothing interesting, memorable, or

engaging about listening to someone run through facts and figures. Unless you are speaking to a boss who is ordering you to speak in a highly unnatural way, you should always strive to narrow the number of key points you present, be conversational (and that means pausing from time to time), and, most importantly, give lots of examples and tell stories to reinforce each major point.

Don't let one impatient boss scar your presenting skills for life.

Wake 'Em Up After Lunch

No matter how brilliant a speaker you are, there are times when people in your audience will fall asleep on you, especially if you are speaking right after lunch. So, what do you do? (The Puritan approach of hitting them over the head to wake them up won't work in most corporate environments.)

One technique I use is to walk right up to the person whose eyes are closed. I will state a general principle that relates to experiences that I feel most people have had in the audience. I will then look directly at the sleeping person and say, "Isn't that right, Jim?" Then, I shake my head up and down.

The sleeping person wakes up instantly and suddenly starts nodding his head and agreeing with me. Then, I quickly turn to someone else

in the audience and start on another point, thereby taking the focus off the snoozing person.

My goal is to wake up the sleepers and put a mild adrenaline rush of fear in the other audience members, so they won't be tempted to fall asleep.

The goal is not to embarrass the audience member, that's why I ask an easy question and steer them into shaking a nod of agreement. That's also why I turn away quickly. The audience member is awake, and the mission accomplished. There's no need to grill him on what he might have missed during the last five minutes.

Now, the rest of your audience will be too afraid to doze off, yet they won't resent you for being a bully because you delicately handled the situation.

Mic Failure Woes

What do you do if you get up to give a speech and you notice that the microphone is cutting in and out on the preceding speaker?

For starters, assess if you really need a mic. If the room has 30 people or fewer, simply project your voice louder than usual and get rid of the mic. You should also get as close as possible to your audience members. This works especially well if you are giving a speech for less than five minutes, as longer than that can be a strain on the voice if you have to project forcefully.

Your second option, if the room is too large (50 to 5,000 people), is to simply speak as you normally would into the microphone. When you hear it cut out, or when you judge from people's expressions that it cut out, just restate your sentence or thought over again. Think of it as though you were translating your speech from one language to another.

Don't apologize. Don't act frustrated. Just do it.

Never call attention to problems, just focus on doing what needs to be done to make the communication happen.

Finally, don't forget to ask for a new mic before it's your turn to speak.

Shout It Out

The hardest venue for most speakers is when you are at a public reception or event in a noisy restaurant or other facility not built for meetings. You have no microphone. There are 50 or more people present, and all are talking. Even if most of them stop talking, it is still difficult for the speaker to be heard.

The problem is that once you start speaking, nobody can hear you. In this case, you must realize that all of the normal rules about speaking don't apply. This means you can't worry about sounding conversational or having a full range of tones and volume in your voice. Instead, you have to worry about one thing only: making yourself heard.

For starters, try to stand in the center of the room so that you are as close as possible to the greatest number of people. Next, take deep breaths and project your voice from the lower abdomen and not just your voice box when you speak. Try to speak as loudly as possible without actually yelling. If you must shout, do so. Your nervousness is likely to make your voice softer and quieter. You must fight this impulse and project even LOUDER.

When it comes to communication, you can't worry about higher levels of skills and impressions if your audience can't hear you. It just won't matter how well you are dressed, how smooth your hand

gestures are, or even how witty your jokes are if people can't hear what you are saying.

First things first. Project loudly or shout so that everyone can hear you.

Chapter 10:
The Top 10 Questions People Ask About Speeches and Presentations

Chapter 10:
The Top 10 Questions
People Ask About Speeches and
Presentations

This is your quick guide to some of the most burning questions about public speaking. These questions are taken from people just like you who have shown up at our workshops or one-on-one trainings. Some come from people who have been presenting for years and years, while others come from those who have just started to realize the importance of building these skills. What's the one thing they all have in common? They knew that they needed to gain the tools contained in this book if they were to move ahead in business, their jobs, and life.

We hope you find this quick reference section helpful and will test the strategies here and throughout the book.

Question 1:

How Can I Get Over Stage Fright And Nervousness Before I Give A Speech?

We've all heard the advice: "Picture your audience naked and they won't seem intimidating," or "Think positive thoughts and you will have a positive impact." But, it just doesn't seem to be enough to do the job of alleviating all those pre-speech jitters. That's because it isn't the best advice.

Here's some shocking information:

The good news: You should be nervous before giving a speech. It means that you are normal! It means that you have a pulse! It means that you care about how the speech or presentation will go.

The bad news: Chances are you are going to bore the heck out of us like most speakers do. This means that you are going to get up and read from a sheet of paper–or worse, read off the PowerPoint screen the entire time. You might even *ignore* the audience. We've all seen people do this. It's no fun to watch, in fact, it's just plain boring.

Here's the solution:

Why don't you try something radical, like actually delivering an interesting, relevant speech full of compelling case studies, stories,

and examples that will help us improve our businesses or lives? Isn't that what the audience really wants? Think about your experience as a listener or audience member. You're not really that interested in the speaker and his or her life. You want good information.

People are not looking for dazzling transitions on the PowerPoint. They want easily relatable information that will help them improve their businesses or lives. You accomplish this by relaying interesting case studies, personal stories or anecdotes, and examples to support what you're saying.

Four steps to overcoming your fear of speaking:

1. Have the tools
2. Practice, practice, practice
3. Have an outline
4. Be an audience-centered speaker, not a me-centered speaker

1. Have the tools

Most people are scared because they lack the tools it takes to know what they are doing when giving a speech. This book is filled with all the tools you'll need to not only look better, sound better, and be more interesting, but also, to give you the confidence that you CAN do it. Here's a question we ask clients all the time when doing an on-site training: Is it better to *look* comfortable and relaxed or *be* comfortable and relaxed?" Although we'd all like to be more

comfortable and relaxed, as far as your audience is concerned, it's better to look more comfortable and relaxed.

2. Practice, practice, practice

Yes, we know that everyone is busy. Most practice time is spent making your PowerPoint longer, or getting everything you plan to say onto the screen so that you don't have to bring a bulleted list to peek at. Is that really what the audience wants – to see you reading your script off of the screen? No!

Here's a way to make practice easy. Write out an outline of what you'd like to say during your speech. Say it out loud at least once. (Sure we'd like to have you practice more, but we're trying to be practical.) Videotape the speech. (Most digital still cameras even have a video function now and can make this part easy.) Play it back and think about the changes you want to make. What happens here is that the first time you give the speech is like your first draft. When you play it back and analyze, it's like your second draft. Even if you get up and deliver it next, it will be essentially your third draft. At least you didn't go out there showing everyone your first rough draft. In business, that would be like sending out a resume that you didn't bother to spell check. That just wouldn't be a wise idea.

3. Have an outline

Please tell me that you're not putting your whole outline in PowerPoint! What happens if the power goes out? What happens if the computer crashes? What happens if the PowerPoint file gets corrupted or is left on another computer?!!

These are all real and unfortunate events that have happened to us, and are all potential problems that can easily be dealt with.

The solution: make an outline on paper. This outline is, ideally, just one page long. No one should see you changing pages. The type size should be 20pts, if possible, so you can see it from a distance. You may wonder, "But what if the audience sees me look at my outline at some point?" It's okay to pause and peek as long as you make sure to make eye contact when it counts: when you're imparting great stories, using interesting examples, and being more interesting and personable than they're used to. The best thing about this outline is that it will never crash, it's portable, it can be placed in a pocket if need be, and it will give you comfort and peace of mind.

4. Be an audience-centered speaker, not a me-centered speaker

This is something we heavily focus on in our trainings. The more you focus inwardly, the more you'll listen to the internal dialogue in your brain. The more you focus on your audience, the more that

stuff starts to dissipate. When you are concerned with *their* needs and wants, your own needs and nervousness goes away.

Question 2:

What Is The Best Way To Begin My Speech?

Here's is a multiple choice question for you. How do you begin your speech?

> A. Tell people how humbled you are by the nice introduction you received.
>
> B. Weave your branding slogan in the first 30 seconds. Then tell people about all of your locations.
>
> C. Say: "Good morning. As you heard, my name is . . . and my title is. . . . I'm happy to be here today. Thank you for that lovely introduction. Before I begin today, let me tell you about the [incredibly boring] history of my company, starting back to its founding in 1923. Next, I'd like to tell you about all of the cities we are in..." (ones you couldn't possibly care about, because you aren't in those cities).
>
> D. None of the above

If you picked '*D – None of the above*,' then you must have experience as an audience member. The other suggestions are not

the worst ideas to begin your speech, but they are tired, boring, and cliché.

What the audience is really thinking and wishing is "please tell us something interesting and relevant. In a way, we kind of unapologetically just care about ourselves. If you address our needs, we'll be more likely to pay attention to the rest of your speech!"

Here are a few ideas that will get the speech fired up from the start:

- Start talking about what the audience is thinking.
- Start talking about what the audience needs.
- Start with the "What's in it for me" element of your speech. The audience needs to know early on what will be important and applicable to them.
- Tell an interesting story that has a relevant point.

Any or all of these suggestions will help you have a killer opening.

Question 3: How Do I Get Rid Of My "Uhs" And "Ums"?

We've heard about all the crazy things people do to get rid of "uhs" and "ums."

Some say to videotape yourself and then stop the tape every time you say "uh" or "um." Or, some suggest counting to "three Mississippi" silently in your head and pause instead of filling the sound with "uh" or "um." Others have someone else ring a bell every time you say "uh" or "um" during a speech. Or, how about the wild idea of being docked ten dollars every time you say one of them? Wouldn't that be a fun way to get you to stop?

Although some of these methods may work for some people, we have tested another method on clients and friends. This alternative method will not humiliate you, frustrate you, or make you broke. We use something we call a "Tic Buster."

Our magical Tic Buster is a card filled with little words we call verbal tics. On the card you'll see "uh," "um," "like," "err" and other equally distracting filler words that somehow habitually make it into people's speech. Stamped over each word is the international, red NO symbol.

In life, we know that the big red circle with the authoritarian slash is a symbol that represents directives and means "no" (no left turn, no parking, and so on.) For our purposes, it now means "NO UM," or any other verbal tic you're having difficulty removing from your speech.

We suggest that you place this symbol on the 12 of your watch, or on your cell phone or computer. Ideally, you want to put it in a spot you look at often each day. The idea here is that the notion of "NO UM" will start to get through to your subconscious. Leave the sticker on for a period of one week. Over the first few days it will work as a visual reminder. You'll still say "uh" or "um," but you will start to catch yourself. Over time, the delay between saying the verbal tic and catching yourself will decrease to the point that you will simply stop *before* saying "um" or "uh" It's seems silly, and very simple… but it works!

Here is the great residual effect:

As you pause, people think that you are about to say something brilliant. As it turns out, "the words that follow [pause] do sound more brilliant," as opposed to: "the words that follow, um, do sound more brilliant."

If you really feel you need extra help and an extra reminder, make a larger version of our "NO UM" symbol and place it on your bathroom mirror. You'll find that this is surprising and helpful as you embark on your journey to eliminate the verbal filler words – those annoying tics.

Want one of our Tic Busters? Call us toll free at 1-800-755-7220. We'll send one your way, no charge.

Question 4:
Should I Take Questions During My Presentation, Or Ask People To Hold Them Until The End?

Here's the one thing you know about your audience members: if they are asking you a question that means they are not falling asleep or Instant Messaging someone. Isn't that a condition you'd like your audience to stay in as often as possible during your presentation?

This topic is covered in greater detail in Chapter 7 of this book. Questions are a good thing. In sales, questions mean that the prospect is getting out all of their potential objections before making a buying decision. Salespeople welcome "objections." You should welcome questions because it moves people closer and closer to "buying" into what it is that you're talking about.

What if you can't answer the question? Oh no, they've stumped you!

I would hope that all of you would have some level of mastery over the topic you are presenting on. If for some reason someone gives you a question that you either don't want to talk about or can't talk about, you should give a short answer to deal with it, and then simply move to a topic that you do know about.

Don't get all flustered, start stuttering, and look embarrassed. Simply say, "You know, I'm not a lawyer, but what I have heard is …" or "Those are statistics our marketing department would have, but what I can tell you is that last year we saw the most growth and I think it was due to…." See, you just segued right back into your expertise. It's an honest way to handle a little ignorance. Don't beat yourself up over it. Don't apologize about not knowing something. You'll learn more and become a better speaker in the end.

Question 5:
How Can I Be More Concise?

Some may say that you should limit your presentation to no more than 10 slides. Others will say that you ought to strip out all of your stories, examples, and anecdotes and just stick to the facts so you will be able to slim down your presentation. Others might even come up with the crazy notion that your audience will lose you if you speak for more than 18.5 seconds!

Concise? Why don't you actually try to tell your audience stuff that's interesting and useful? If you do that, the time will fly and they won't be staring at their watches, wondering what time is lunch. If your speech is a concise nine minutes long but you are reading from your slides and being boring, your audience may tune-out after just 30 seconds, and the next eight and a half minutes will seem like three hours!

So what did you really accomplish? Guess what? Your audience will never complain about someone not being concise if they are really interesting – even if they talk for three hours.

To really make a presentation concise, try narrowing your messages to only three key points. (Your audience can really only remember three to five messages anyway.) Add some brief stories and examples that truly illustrate those messages. Then test it. See how

your audience reacts. What we have found is that they are more awake, more engaged, and more apt to remember and act on what was said. In fact, let us know the results of your own tests. Email us at Jess@MediaTrainingWorldwide.com. Everyday we hear back from people we've trained on techniques they have tried. We want to hear from you, too.

Question 6:
What Should I Do With My Hands?

Simply put, use your hands! We train different groups from all over the world. It's just more interesting to listen to speakers who are conversational and don't look and sound like "stiffs." Our favorite speakers both sound and look like they are talking to their best friend at a bar. Have you ever noticed people talking to friends in a casual setting? Guess what, whether you realize it or not, we all move our hands a lot.

Helpful "handy" tips:

- Don't lock your hands down on a lectern
- Don't hold papers, pens, and remotes while speaking
- Don't clasp your hands in front of you
- Don't clasp your hands behind you

- *DO* keep your hands out so that they are free to move in unison with the points you're trying to make

Still unconvinced that you'll look more relaxed and confident moving your hands? Take any one-minute section from your speech and test it. Videotape it first with hand movement, and then again without hand movement. Get someone else to look at it. Don't tell them what you were doing different. Just ask which one was better. Then ask them why.

Question 7:
How Many PowerPoint Slides And Bullet Points Should I Use In My Entire PowerPoint Presentation?

Here are some things you may have heard from other people:

"Let's use no more than 30 slides. We got criticism for the old presentation we did with 50 slides."

"10! The magic answer is 10. Thou shalt use no more and no fewer than 10 slides. 10 is the perfect number."

"The more slides I prepare, the smarter and more well-prepared I'll look. I'll try to limit the slides to 50, but if I put more in, people can use the PowerPoint as a resource in their office for the next year."

Ok, here's the real answer:

The correct number of slides could be one, or it could be 100 (or it could be zero.) If a slide will help your audience understand and remember the message better, then use it. If not, don't use *any* slides. Follow that principle and the number of slides issue will take care of itself.

And, as for bullet points, there is no hard empirical evidence that says people will learn better if you put your notes on a screen and make them read while you talk. We recommend that you ask yourself the same question when creating a PowerPoint: "Will this slide help my audience understand and remember the message better?" If so, then use it.

We find that audiences tend to remember images rather than text. Are there pictures you have or could find that would help make your messages come alive?

Of course, if there is important text based information to be disseminated to your listeners, you can – and should – give it to them in the form of a handout. They can then take it with them are

read it over later to refresh their memory. However using interesting images are, as a rule, more interesting, inspiring, and compelling than laundry lists of dry information.

Question 8:

Is It Okay To Read From My PowerPoint Slides?

"What?!! How insulting that you would read to us! Maybe you could read us a bedtime story later, too! Either way, you'll be putting us to sleep or, at the very least, encourage us to day dream!"

Do you want to lose your audience right away? The following are a few things that happen when you read to an audience:

- They instantly know what kind of presenter you are… a lazy one. You've just put your notes on the screen instead of coming up with bullet points, knowing where you'd like to go in your speech, and just plain talking to us!

- You are forcing the audience to make a decision: read or listen to you speak. People just can't do both effectively.

- Watching you read is actually less fun than watching paint dry.

So what do you do? How do you give a presentation without putting the words you plan to say on screen?

First, write an outline of what you'd like to talk about. Next, think of stories and examples for each. Finally, ask yourself are there pictures or images that would enhance each message you plan to talk about? If so, get them and put them in your presentation – then ditch the text. If you can't think of any visuals... don't have a slide. Your audience doesn't want to read it, and they certainly don't want to watch you read either.

Question 9:
How Will I Know If My Speech "Worked?"

Do you need expensive focus groups?

Do you need to invest in a Magic 8 Ball to tell you if it worked?

Do you need to wait until someone asks you for your autograph?

NO.

There's a very simple and effective way to test and *know* if your speech works. Just ask your audience members.

Chances are that someone will come up to you after your speech and tell you that you were great. (They might mean it, they might not). This is the perfect opportunity to really test whether or not your speech was effective. Ask them specifically, "what it was that they remembered and took away from the speech." If they simply say, "Everything about your speech was great," that means nothing you said was memorable and your speech was a complete failure. However, if they refer to a compelling story, or a memorable slide that stuck in their brain, now you know that it worked!

Continue to refine and test you speech, keeping what people remember and changing what they don't.

Question 10:
How Should I End My Speech?

Nothing is worse than a speaker who just quickly and abruptly finishes the last bullet point on a presentation and says "that's-it-any-questions-thank-you-and-goodbye" as they dart off the stage.

End with a purpose. End with finality in your voice. End with a little inspiration.

Don't throw us off-guard. Don't end like a car that was going down the highway at 70 miles per hour and then suddenly runs out of gas. You don't have to be funny or poignant, but at least do this:

- Restate your main points, summarize, or ask the audience to do something. ("Call to action")
- Leave them with one final thought – and that thought should NOT be that you are desperate to get out of the room!
- Give the audience members some sort of nod or signal that this is, in fact, the end. If an audience is unsure, they won't clap or act appropriately.
- Leave them well-informed, interested, and charged-up. In short, leave the audience members happy!

Just like any warm and fuzzy kind of story, try to impart with your audience on a happily-ever-after feeling that they can take away!

Conclusion

If you want to become a better speaker, you need to make a lifetime commitment. Analyze every speaker you see in the future from two perspectives: (1) substance and content, and (2) style and form. You should constantly assess what you like and don't like about the style of each speaker in which you come into contact. When someone bores you, take notes and vow not to repeat the same blunders. When someone is captivating, take even more detailed notes on EXACTLY what he or she does, and try to borrow whatever techniques you feel comfortable repeating.

Additionally, you should video and audiotape all of your presentations in the future, then watch or listen to them. If you do this regularly, you will become a better communicator every year.

Good luck!

Additional Resources

Public Workshops
A 2 day intensive course that teaches you how to be a powerful communicator every time you speak to any audience.
www.presentationtrainingworkshop.com

One-on-One Presentation Training
Learn to become a better speaker in lightning speed with One On One Training.
www.oneononespeechtraining.com

Corporate or Private Training
Do you have more than one person who needs training? Invite the sales team or PR Department… We customize the training to meet your needs – no matter the size.
www.privatespeakingtraining.com

Media Training
Look your best, sound your best, and get quoted saying what you want.
www.privatemediatraining.com

Training Products
DVDs, CDs, Books… Almost everything related to improving your communication skills can be found in our online store.
www.mediatrainingworldwide.com/store/

Online Training
Powered by ULiveandLearn.com, a trusted name in the online training industry, this online course follows the techniques found in this book. However, it adds video, audio, and interactive enhancements to help you develop and further improve your presentation skills.
www.presentationtrainingschool.com

Free Videos

Watch a free training video about improving your presentation skills.

www.freespeakervideo.com

The Speaking Channel

The Speaking Channel is a news and how-to information source covering speaking, presentation and oral communication skills. New videos are broadcast daily.

www.speakingchannel.tv

Voice Spray

Have you ever lost your voice or suffered from laryngitis? Imagine never losing your voice or getting laryngitis again, or even going hoarse.

www.tjsvoicesave.com

TV Friendly Ties

Made to look good on TV, without distracting from your message.

www.tjstvties.com

TV Makeup for Men

Everyone on TV has makeup on. Be prepared for every situation.

www.tjstvmakeup.com

About Media Training Worldwide

Media Training Worldwide provides more media and presentation training workshops and seminars than any other company in the world. Media Training Worldwide also publishes more than 100 media and presentation training books, DVDs, CDs and other informational products and is the premier presentation/media training publisher in the world.

At Media Training Worldwide, we specialize in media, presentation, public speaking and speech training, as well as executive coaching, to enhance verbal and non-verbal communication skills for media interview, presentations, and public speaking. We provide two-day, one- day, half-day, teleseminar and showcase media and presentation training programs to fit any budget or timeframe. We will bring our video equipment and expertise directly to you, anywhere in the world. Many clients prefer to train in our New York City-Times Square based TV and Presentation training studio, which features satellite TV interview backdrops, TelePrompTers, lecterns, large TV monitors, talk show sets, PowerPoint projectors, screens, board room settings, and even virtual reality audiences! We can simulate any media or presentation situation you may encounter.

At Media Training Worldwide we specialize exclusively in media training, presentation training and public speaking training/coaching. That's all we do. We eat, think and sleep media training and presentation coaching.

The result?

We provide the highest level of service to you and guarantee that your communication skills will improve dramatically because you will be using the most innovative training and learning techniques and technologies available.

Visit Us Online
www.mediatrainingworldwide.com

More About The Authors

TJ Walker,
Media Training Worldwide CEO

TJ Walker, CEO of Media Training Worldwide, is one of the leading authorities on media and presentation training in the world. With more than 20 years of media training experience, Walker has trained thousands of CEOs, authors, and experts, including leading government officials in the United States, European Prime Ministers, and African diplomats. He is producer and host of daily audio and video Speakcast broadcasts covering media and presentation training tips and techniques and owner and producer of the Speaking Channel TV Network.

Jess Todtfeld,
Media Training Worldwide President

Jess Todtfeld, President of Media Training Worldwide, is one of the leading speaking and media training authorities in the U.S. With more than 15 years of experience, Todtfeld helps CEOs, business executives, spokespeople, public relations representatives, experts, and authors not just become better speakers, but become expert speakers.

Prior to joining Media Training Worldwide, Todtfeld founded Success In Media, Inc., and brings with him 15 years of experience as a Television Producer on the National Level. During that time he booked and produced over 4,000 segments, including those at cable TV's #1 news channel, FOX NEWS CHANNEL and with cable's #1 prime time show, "The O'Reilly Factor" with Bill O'Reilly.

BULLY PULPITS
Speaking Secrets of World Famous Leaders

TJ Walker will entertain, educate and inspire your audience by showing brief video clips of world famous speakers. Then, he analyzes exactly what the speaker is doing well in order to connect and communicate with the audience. This daily show takes you behind the scenes to see exactly how famous leaders communicate effectively. Walker shares the same analysis with the audience that he normally shares in private when coaching world leaders.

You will walk away with practical information and tips on how to communicate more effectively in your next presentation AND will be inspired to improve to the next level of speaking, from the boardroom to the convention hall.

Sample Spotlight Speakers:

Teddy Roosevelt	Joel Osteen	Michael Dell
Steve Jobs	Billy Graham	Jack Valenti
Ronald Reagan	Oprah Winfrey	Gordon Moore
Jack Welch	Suzi Orman	Barbra Streisand
Carly Fiorina	Barbara Walters	Mark Cuban
Winston Churchill	Warren Buffet	Richard Branson
Martin Luther King	Norman Vincent	Golda Meir
John F. Kennedy	Peale	Donald Trump
Robert F. Kennedy	Stephen Covey	Zig Ziglar
Steve Ballmer	Nelsen Mandela	And many moe...

www.SpeakingChannel.tv

Also available as a keynote speech
www.speakingkeynote.com